LOVE, LUST & FAKING IT

ALSO BY JENNY McCARTHY

JEN-X

BELLY LAUGHS

BABY LAUGHS

LIFE LAUGHS

LOUDER THAN WORDS

MOTHER WARRIORS

HEALING AND PREVENTING AUTISM

LOVE, LUST & FAKING IT

The Naked Truth About Sex, Lies, and True Romance

Jenny McCarthy

HARPER

An Imprint of HarperCollinsPublishers
www.harpercollins.com

Names and identifying details of some individuals
have been changed to protect their privacy.

HarperCollins books may be purchased for educational, business, or sales promotional use.
For information, please write: Special Markets Department, HarperCollins Publishers, 10
East 53rd Street, New York, NY 10022.

FIRST EDITION

Library of Congress Cataloging-in-Publication Data

McCarthy, Jenny, 1972-
    Love, lust & faking it : the naked truth about sex, lies, and true romance /
Jenny McCarthy. -- 1st ed.
        p.   cm.
    ISBN 978-0-06-201298-2
    1. Women--Sexual behavior. 2. Lust. I. Title.
HQ29.M455 2010
306.7082--dc22

                                                            2010024941

10 11 12 13 14 OV/RRD 10 9 8 7 6 5 4 3 2 1

Thank you for trusting *the key*.

It's okay to open the door.

The dream is real.

Contents

Part Three: Faking It . . .

Part One

LOVE . . .

Finding Your First Love

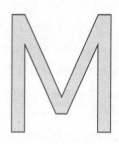y parents were married for thirty years. And I thought for sure they would never get divorced. Not because they publicly adored each other or looked at each other with meaningful looks—quite the contrary. I thought they would stay together forever because divorce happened to other people, not my family. But it did happen, and they divorced when I was twenty-one. I knew it was better off that way, but I still crawled into bed and gave it a good old cry.

I couldn't possibly imagine my parents with new boyfriends or girlfriends. Gross! It made me sick to my stomach to even think of them getting naughty with someone else. But after a year or so of my parents being "on the market," my mom called with an amazing story from her past. There was this boy named Tom who she dated from the time she was fifteen to age twenty. Tom was her high school sweetheart. They went to each other's proms and have pictures to prove their growth through puberty together. They were madly in love with one another, until one horrific day . . .

My mom found a picture of another girl in Tom's wallet, not even a naked one, and she freaked the hell out. Tom swore to my mom it was only in there because the girl gave it to him, and that was it. Mom didn't believe him, of course, and threw him out. She was devastated and avoided Tom at every cost. Tom didn't give up, though. He knocked on doors, showed up at her work, and tried everything aside from handing her a gift box with his balls in it to get Mom back. Mom then quickly started dating this guy named Dan, who happens to be my dad. He had just returned from serving in Vietnam, and was after my mom like she was a hot little cupcake. As my mom put it, they were waiting to have sex until they were married, so they decided to tie the knot in a matter of months. The wedding was set and was a week away. But she felt sad; it just didn't feel right. Tom showed up that night and said, "Please don't do this. I love you, Linda, you're my life, don't marry that guy." Mom started bawling her eyes out and said, "I'm sorry, but my mom already paid for the wedding."

They both cried, and then she did what she had to do: she threw him out of the house as fast as she could. She knew he was the love of her life, but there was nothing she could do about it. They never saw each other again. Ugh! That killed me. I couldn't believe that for thirty years my mom's heart had been in another place!

As soon as she finished telling me this story, I started freaking out. How romantic! I mean, the part about not really wanting to marry my dad was a little upsetting, but this sounded like the love of her life. I told her that we should try to find him—maybe he was divorced, too. Pretty much all the baby boomers were divorced, so I thought her odds were pretty great.

She replied, "I did find him."

To give you a little backstory, my mom worked as a janitor in a courthouse. Yes, a janitor. She cleaned up jail cells and bathrooms and actually enjoyed her job. That's just how living saints roll, I guess. Apparently she'd been cleaning a courtroom the day before, and a lawyer came back because he forgot his briefcase. She looked up, and it was Tom. They both stared at each other in silence for a second. My mom uttered, "Tom?" It was like the Luke and Laura reunion on *General Hospital*, but without the male perm. They slowly approached each other in shock. She said he looked exactly the same, except he was bald. She said they talked about how long it had been and compared notes on their families. Then my mom dropped the "I'm divorced" card, just to see what he would say. Tom replied, "I'm separated from my wife." DING DING DING!

I said, "Mom, it's meant to be. This is the love of your life! I can't believe you guys found each other like this." But being more Catholic than the pope, my mom replied, "Well, I can't pursue anything until he's completely divorced."

I begged her to at least go to dinner. She already believed she was going to burn in hell anyway for getting a divorce from my dad, so I said, "Why not just be naughty, since you're already going to hell?" She laughed, and I was able to hear in her voice an excitement I hadn't heard in years.

Mom and Tom were married in April 2000 and are still going strong. They talk about "doing it," and it completely grosses me out. But I'm happy she's happy. As for my dad, he's still single. Please write to me if your mom is looking for a guy who can dance like a spider monkey with a little too much whisky in him.

In the meantime, Facebook your first love. Hopefully he doesn't look like Don Rickles!

My Endless Love

fter sharing my mom's story, I couldn't help but tell you about my first love. As I close my eyes, I bring up a memory that I can share from my heart. This one comes immediately to mind. . . .

"No! Please don't leave me!" I shouted, as I clung to Tony LoBianco's sixteen-year-old leg. Tony had caught me talking to one of his football teammates, Bob Caponigro, and wanted to break up with me because of it. Tony was my everything: my life, my breath, my smile, and my reason for wearing cherry lip gloss after school. He didn't wind up breaking up with me at this particular moment, but his urge to start "checking out more meat at the deli" was about to rear its ugly head.

"I think we should break up for a month," said Tony. "I want to go on spring break, and need to feel free." At this point we had been dating for four years (which is twenty-eight years in teenager years), and the love of my life had just asked to break up with me for a month so he could be free on spring break. Could there be a worse thing to say to a sixteen-year-old girl who just had her cherry popped by him the year before? I mean, what the hell? I immediately fell to the ground in hysterics.

"No, please don't do this! I'll die." I tried grabbing his leg once again, but he was able to break free. I watched Tony walk out the door with a spring in his step, excited to meet some spring break canooters!

I lay in my bed for the next four weeks, unable to go to school, to eat, or to speak. My parents thought I had had a psychotic break. I kept dreaming about how things used to be between us. Watching Tony pretend to be my dad on the phone to call in sick to school for me, so we could hump all over his house. Picking a song as "our" song that we thought would be played on the radio for a century. (We decided on "Endless Love" by Diana Ross and Lionel Richie. We thought that one would play in grocery stores for the rest of our lives—and we were right.) We talked about the children we would have together, and what we would name them: Lionel, Diana, and Brooke. We were one of those couples that everyone in school talked about: "Jenny and Tony are going to be in love forever."

Nothing will ever come close to matching the voltage of your first love in terms of intensity. Kind of like with sex. Nothing later will ever be able to top the first time a guy has sex—that HOLY CRAP WHAT THE HELL WAS THAT?!?! Well, that's what first true love feels like to a girl. Tony was my first everything. My first make-out session, my first dry hump, my first finger, my first boob squeeze, my first hickey, my first BJ . . . you get the idea. Tony was it for me. If he hadn't walked out on me to go on spring break, I would have been the most faithful, wonderful, childbearing, respectful wife to him for the rest of my life.

But looking back now, I couldn't be more grateful that Tony wanted a spring break hookup. During those four weeks of crying in bed in a catatonic state, something shifted inside me. The perfect Catholic, obedient sweet girl named Jenny grew the beginning part of a backbone while dying in that bed. I don't know how, but the shift had slowly begun.

Tony came back from spring break, and I did what any love-starved sixteen-year-old girl would do—I took him back. Then, after a week of making up, he dropped another bomb on me. Tony had met a girl that he "kissed" on spring break, and had invited her to be his date to prom! Tony said he felt bad because the girl had already bought her dress. Needless to say, I was shocked. I had been dating Tony since I was twelve! Mind you, we didn't break up; I just made him promise not to touch her the entire night. My prom wasn't until the next year, so I had to sit at home and drink Bacardi until I puked green and it was over. Tony came back to me with his promises that nothing happened at prom, and we continued to date.

Now I know what you're thinking: Where's that backbone you spoke of, that shift? Well just you wait, it's coming.

We continued to date for a year. Many back-seat parking-lot sex sessions, lots of cuddling. Then spring break time rolled around again. This was now my senior year of high school, and Tony was a freshman in college. I sat him down one night and said, "This is my one and only spring break in my lifetime. I would like to break up for four weeks and experience spring break feeling free." The look on his face was heartbreaking. I wasn't doing this as revenge; I just felt that if I were going to marry Tony someday, I wanted to have the same life experiences he did. He walked out of my house crushed. I felt bad, but I was excited to experience some spring break meatheads!

When I got back from spring break, with my sunburned skin peeling off my face, Tony and I immediately got back together. I just had to break it to him that I met a guy on spring break that I "kissed" and had invited to my prom. Déjà vu, but I didn't care; I wanted fairness in this relationship. So . . . Bobbie from Long Island flew out and took me to the prom, while it was Tony's turn to stay home and chug rum. My prom turned out to be a disaster—all Bobbie wanted to do was squeeze my boobs.

Once that nightmare was over, Tony and I continued our relationship, and it was stronger than ever. We'd both gotten to see what it was like with someone else for a whole four weeks, and were coming up on our seventh anniversary. But a few days before I turned nineteen, I woke up feeling like I was meant to be moving on. I guess the seven-year itch had set in. I was still deeply, deeply in love with Tony, but I felt a yearning to go see the world. I told him to meet me at White Castle on the corner of Seventy-ninth and Pulaski. I sat in my car as I watched him walk down the street toward me. My eyes filled with tears, thinking about how I had gotten to watch this boy turn into a man. We had spent the most important years of our lives together. We were Tony and Jenny . . . and I was about to officially end it.

He jumped in my car with a solemn look. "You're ending it, aren't you?"

"Yes," I cried. I said, "for no other reason than it's time for me to go. I love you, Tony. I'll always love you."

I climbed on top of him, and we held each other and cried. After about thirty minutes, he kissed me on the cheek and got out of the car, and I watched him walk away. That was the last time I ever saw Tony LoBianco.

I suffered through many bad relationships after Tony, and after my marriage ended, I came to the conclusion that true love isn't real. And then I flashed back to Tony. That was real. That was the most real love anyone could experience in a lifetime. So I told myself, I will recognize true love again when a guy can make me feel like Tony LoBianco did.

I still wonder about Tony LoBianco. I have tried to look him up on Facebook and Twitter. No luck. I would love to see him again and tell him, "I meant what I said in White Castle. I'll always love you. You'll always be my Endless Love."

Getting Dumped

Getting dumped might be one of the most painful experiences next to giving birth. Not only do you feel out of control, you feel worthless. Almost everyone has or will experience getting dumped in their lifetime. Unless, of course, you're a nun. Jesus can't dump nuns.

I will never forget a specific "getting dumped" moment in my life. I was shocked and totally blindsided by this experience. I was so caught up in myself and my own problems that I didn't read the signs that problems were escalating in the relationship. I will forever be scarred by the experience. This was the note I came home to one horrific evening.

Jenny,

I can't do this anymore. I feel used and I feel like you don't appreciate me. We've been together for so long and you seem to only care about yourself. You're controlling and I never feel like I get a say in what we do. You come home from work and who is there to take care of you??? I AM!! Who makes you feel good when you're sad? I DO! I've never flaked on you once. I've had my occasional episodes of exhaustion but after I recharged my batteries I was there for you. You need to be more considerate and not take advantage of me the way you do. I feel abused and frankly, I'm ready to find someone else.

P.S. You really need counseling.

The letter was signed, "Your Vibrator." I was in shock that Vibrator had just dumped me. How dare he just abandon me like this? I looked around the house in disbelief that he had really left. It was true. I couldn't find him anywhere. The house was so painfully quiet that I turned on all the ceiling fans just to fill the void and to simulate the humming sound I missed so very much. I read the letter again to try and read into what went wrong. I closed my eyes and looked back into my memory file to recapture the moments that led to this.

When I first met Vibrator, we were at a store. He was staring at me, and I couldn't keep my eyes off of him. He was so much better looking than all the other vibrators. He knew it, too. I could tell by the vibe he put off that this one was meant for me. I approached him slowly.

"Hello Vibrator."

"Wuz up," he replied.

He was cocky. That turned me on even more.

I whispered, "Do you think you can handle a woman like me?"

"Bitch, you have no idea what I'm capable of," he replied.

I ripped him off the shelf and gave him a squeeze.

"I guess we're about to find out, huh?"

That night was our first night together. I screamed in delight as he instinctively knew exactly where my buttons were. After hours of passion, I collapsed onto my pillow and lit a cigarette.

"You're so damn hot," I said to Vibrator.

"I know," he replied.

As months went on, our sex life was beyond passionate. I brought him on trips with me and even bought him new accessories. Vibrator seemed to be happy, but I guess I missed the signs of it being ONLY about sex.

I came home from work one day and found Vibrator on the phone with an abuse victims hotline. I yelled, "Hang up the phone right now or I will knock those batteries right out of your ass!"

Vibrator slammed the phone down and screamed, "Bitch, you don't love me. You never have. I'm exhausted all the time, and I don't feel appreciated for everything I do for you."

Then, Vibrator walked toward the front door. I yelled, "Where the hell do you think you're going?" He replied, "I'm going bowling," and then slammed the door shut. That should have been a lesson for me, but I ignored it and went on with my life.

The next relationship misstep took place in the bathroom. I looked in the tub one afternoon to find Vibrator! My son, Evan, must have mistaken him for a new toy. I yanked him out of the tub. He was choking on water.

"Oh my God, are you okay? I'm so sorry. He thought you were a speedboat."

Cough, cough. "No shit he thought I was a speedboat. You're such an irresponsible bitch."

"Me? Why aren't you in the drawer?"

"Because I'm tired of hiding. I need to be free. You used to take me on trips. Now I just sit here and hear the sounds of *Dancing with the Stars* from a distance, knowing you're sitting on the couch watching it without me."

"I'm sorry. You're right. I know it's your favorite show. I promise I'll TiVo it if I can't have you watch it with me."

The next day I had to go to New York. I knew if I didn't take Vibrator with me, it would be over. So off we went to the airport. As I walked through security, I heard a man shout, "Whose bag is this?" My heart stopped. Oh no, Vibrator. You've been detected. I forgot to remove your batteries. I sheepishly replied, "Mine." The security agent said, "Open your bag, please?"

I stood there in silence. I didn't know how to respond. What if they took Vibrator away from me? "Yes, you can open it," I replied. He opened the bag and saw Vibrator staring at him. The security agent looked at me with an inquisitive look on his face. I calmly said, "It's my boyfriend. Don't take him from me." The agent looked at me like I was crazy and then zipped up my bag. We made it through! Close one. Sadly though, that trip to New York was a disaster. Vibrator's batteries died, and the hotel gift shop was closed. I frantically searched the room and discovered two AA batteries inside the remote control. They were weak. Vibrator sounded like he had had a stroke.

"Whhhat the f*ck isssss wung wit me?" asked Vibrator.

"They don't have anything else. I can't help you till tomorrow. I'm so sorry. I should have been more prepared," I replied.

"I'm breakingggg upt wit you," he said.

"Don't be such a jerk," I replied.

Vibrator got up and stumbled out of the room. Later he e-mailed me . . .

Dear Jenny,
I think the Alicia Keys "Fallin' " song says it best . . .

Sometimes I love ya, uhh, sometimes you make me blue
Sometimes I feel good, at times I feel USED!!!!!

Needless to say, I was confused. I couldn't tell if he was over me or if he was still in love with me. When I got back to L.A., I discovered the break-up note. Vibrator did indeed dump me. Every day I wonder what happened to him. Did he find someone else? Did he find love? I'm still devastated by this abrupt ending. All I wish now is that Vibrator has found a good life. After all, even vibrators deserve happy endings.

[4]

Why Do We Love Who We Love?

Okay, neuroscience world: here's some scientific evidence as to why we love the people we love. I watched this doctor by the name of Dr. Helen Fisher in one of those TED conferences online and was fascinated by what she found. How many times have we wondered why we walked into a room and fell in love with that particular dude over all the other dudes? I made a call and asked her to spill the beans on her research.

JENNY: How do I describe your title?

DR. FISHER: Research Professor, Department of Anthropology, Rutgers University.

JENNY: Wow, that sounds so much better then my 1994 Playboy Playmate of the Year title.

DR. FISHER: (*Chuckles.*)

JENNY: What made you decide to look into the science behind why we love whom we love?

DR. FISHER: I had written my book, *Why We Love*, and I studied the brain circuitry of romantic love and because of it match.com called me two days before Christmas and asked me, "Why do you fall in love with one person rather than another?" And at the time I said, "I don't know." And that set me on this course of looking at some of the brain circuitry of why you're drawn to one person rather than another.

JENNY: Do we tend to fall in love with someone similar to ourselves?

DR. FISHER: Yes, generally we fall in love with someone from the same socioeconomic background, same general level of intelligence, same general level of good looks, same religious and social values, your childhood plays a role. But I wanted to know if body chemistry plays a role. People will say, "Well, we had chemistry or we didn't have chemistry." And I thought to myself, Well, what do they mean by that? Maybe there is some chemistry that pulls us to one person rather than another, and that started me in on my whole thing.

JENNY: Your discovery led you to create these different personality types. They totally made sense to me. Can you explain them to everyone else?

DR. FISHER: I think we've evolved four very broad personality styles associated with the brain chemicals: dopamine, serotonin, testosterone, and the last one is estrogen and oxytocin. I call these personality styles the Explorer, the Builder, the Director, and the Negotiator.

JENNY: Okay, start with the Explorer.

DR. FISHER: Explorers are people who are expressive of the dopamine system. They tend to be novelty seeking, risk taking, spontaneous, energetic, curious, creative, adaptable, flexible, often very liberal.

JENNY: That's so me. Okay, now tell me about the Builder.

DR. FISHER: The Builder is expressive of the serotonin system and tends to be traditional, conventional, cautious but not scared, social, they've got more close friends, they're networking people, they're managerial, they're loyal, they're conscientious, they tend to be concrete thinkers, literal thinkers, they follow the rules, they respect authority.

JENNY: Yeah, that is not me. That's why I had a hard time in Catholic school. I couldn't follow the rules and didn't have much respect for evil nuns.

DR. FISHER: The third is the Director, and it is expressive of the testosterone system; women as well as men Directors tend to be analytical, logical, direct, decisive, tough-minded, good at what we call will-based systems in science—things like math, engineering, computers, mechanics; they tend to be skeptical, they're ambitious, they're rank oriented, they're competitive, they like to debate, they focus deeply but narrowly, and they contain their emotions.

JENNY: And what about the fourth?

DR. FISHER: The Negotiator is expressive of the estrogen and oxytocin system; they tend to see the big picture, they're imaginative, they're intuitive, they've got good verbal skills and people skills, they're emotionally expressive, they're altruistic, nurturing.

JENNY: Aren't we all a little of these?

DR. FISHER: Yes, I think that we're all a combination of all of these, but we have personalities and we express some more than others. The standard, very feminine one is the Negotiator, but there are a lot of women that are the Explorer type and the Builder type.

JENNY: So because I am an Explorer type, would I only be attracted to Explorers?

DR. FISHER: Well, there are two parts to a personality. There's your temperament, which is what I study, your biology, and your character, which comes from your cultural upbringing. Let's say you were an Explorer that grew up with an alcoholic father and everything was chaos and unpredictable and recklessness and you decided you didn't want somebody who was that way. Just because of your upbringing. So you marry a Builder instead, and after about five years you might get bored.

JENNY: Indeed.

DR. FISHER: So, I mean, there's much more to personalities than temperament. About 50 percent of who you are is temperament, but anyway, on the dating site www .chemistry.com, I studied about one thousand people, and yes, Explorers do tend to be attracted to other Explorers. They want somebody equally curious, equally creative, equally energetic.

JENNY: So what about those Builders?

DR. FISHER: Builders do tend to be attracted to other Builders; traditional goes with traditional.

JENNY: That makes sense.

DR. FISHER: But the third and fourth categories, high testosterone tends to go for high estrogen, and high estrogen tends to go for high testosterone. I think a good example is Hillary and Bill Clinton, and Hillary is very high testosterone and she goes for Bill, who is clearly high estrogen.

JENNY: I'm sure Bill will love to hear that! But Bill and Hillary are a really good example that you can mix and match. So they can mix and match?

DR. FISHER: Oh my goodness, of course! I mean, what I've stumbled on is some basic patterns of nature that dopamine goes for dopamine, serotonin goes for serotonin; testosterone goes for estrogen and vice versa. However, there are huge variations on them, for example, take the guy who's been around the block a million times and had sex with everybody and is very much the explorer type, curious about everything, they get into their late thirties and suddenly want to settle down, and who do they choose? A Builder who offers home and family and stability and community. So you know, many many many things play a role in mate choice. But what I'm trying to add is really the dramatic role of temperament, biology.

JENNY: Well all I can say is . . . I can't wait to explore some Explorers!!

DR. FISHER: Enjoy!

5

Prove Your Love: Tattoo It!

Thursdays in college were called "nickel draft nights." A beer was seriously five cents. That was a good thing, considering I only had fifty cents in my pocket most of the time. Once when I was a sophomore, I was determined to get drunk and felt up. After my fourth beer I realized I was not even close to being buzzed yet. I needed at least twenty more cents to achieve the perfect set of beer goggles. Then it happened. "Can I buy you a beer?" Wow. This big spender was cute, and I wasn't even wasted yet. And he was buying me a beer. Two points for him! He threw down a nickel, and I downed another drink. Then he threw down another nickel, and I downed another one. Fifteen cents later I found myself pressed up against the wall with my tongue down his throat.

"Wanna walk back to my place?" he slurred. "Hell yeah," is what I vaguely remember answering. We stumbled out of the bar and walked down the main street. My stomach was feeling woozy, so I slurred, "Let's get a pizza slice to soak up the booze. I don't want to puke on you." He agreed and held on to me, not to help me walk but because he was holding himself up using my body. When we arrived at the pizza place there was a line so we were forced to stare at the drunk people in the tattoo shop next door. "Look at those idiots getting tattoos," I said. My drunken dude replied, "I wonder how much it costs, I always wanted to get one."

Now let me just pause the story for a moment to tell you something about me in college. I was the one who said, "F*ck it," and did what most people wouldn't do. If my friends needed someone to test pills they found in a drawer, I volunteered. If people needed someone to drive cross-country with them to visit a boyfriend, I jumped in the car and drove with them. This was, without a doubt, the fallout from going to Catholic school for twelve years. I wanted to be free from rules and went against everything that I "shouldn't" do. So, I hear this cute drunk guy say, "I always wanted to get one," and of course I reply, "Let's do it. I got a few bucks left on my credit card." He pushed me against the wall for another deep throat session with his tongue. I guess he really wanted a tattoo. After a hot, wet kiss he said, "You're the coolest chick ever. Let's get a tattoo that matches each other." I replied with the most romantic response I could muster, which was, "F*ck yeah."

We opened the door to the tattoo parlor and began looking for permanent art to immortalize this moment. In my drunken stupor I remember looking at him, thinking, I think I love this drunk dude. He pointed to a symbol on the wall and said, "How about that one?" It was a yin-yang symbol. For those who don't know, it's a Chinese symbol that represents how things work. One half of the circle is dark and the other side is white. They symbolize good and bad and together they balance each other. He said, "Why don't we each get one side of the symbol? That way when we're together we are balanced as one." I almost died! This man standing before me was so deep. He was like Yoda, only much cuter. (Looking back now, I realize that it wasn't spiritual insight; he probably had just finished watching a Steven Seagal movie.) I took my credit card out and paid for both of our tattoos.

He was up first and took it like a champ. I hopped up on the table and stared into his eyes, thinking this guy might just be the one. As the needle zapped my skin I felt a rush of excitement flow through my body. I knew it went against all of the moral issues I had growing up. My mom hated tattoos, and the fact that it was a symbol outside Catholicism would make her hit the rosary even harder than when I got a hickey. I looked at the drunk guy and smiled. "Together we are one"—how cool is that, I kept thinking. As blood dripped down my lower back I became woozy. I never had gotten that slice of pizza to soak up the booze, and the evidence of that projected out of my mouth all over the floor. This didn't seem to shock anyone. It was late, everyone was drunk, and a mop came out of nowhere, erasing the evidence in seconds. I smiled coyly and said, "Whoops." Cute drunk guy didn't care. I was his yin and he was my yang.

The tattoo was complete and we stood next to each other with our butts facing the mirror. The tattoo was on our lower backs so when we stood next to each other it made a circle. My half completed his half. Someone walked by us and looked and said in the most perfect Chelsea Handler delivery, "That's the dumbest tattoo I have ever seen. Are you guys gay?" We looked at each other and lowered our tops. Oh my God, what had I just done? Was I just drunk, or was I caught up in the romance of permanent ink love? I went back to my apartment and passed out. The next day I showed my roommates, and they confirmed how stupid my tattoo looked. "Idiot, it looks like a sperm without the other half of the yang." I was so humiliated.

A month later I went back home to visit my mom and caught the stomach flu. I was vomiting into the toilet, and my shirt bunched up. The next thing I know, my mom started screaming and whacking me with her hand because she saw my tattoo. "For the love of Jesus Christ, Jenny, you got a tattoo!" I cried out, "Mom, ouch! Please stop hitting me, I'm puking!"

"What in the h-e-l-l is that thing?" she yelled. "It's a yin-yang," I replied. "Is it a devil thing?" she yelled again. "No, Mom, it means balance." She replied, "It looks like a sperm!"

In case you're wondering, I never got the tattoo removed, and I have had to answer the question, "What in the hell is that sperm doing on your back?" for almost twenty years.

I'm not against tattoos after this experience. I dig 'em and really want to get one I like in this lifetime, but what I would like to remind people is that there seems to be a curse (at least in Hollywood)—when you tattoo someone's name on you or share a symbol, it never seems to work out.

I have often wondered what the drunk guy thinks about sharing a tattoo with me for all these years. Who knows, maybe we'll bump into each other again. After all, he is my yang.

6

How to Love Yourself: A Lesson from Byron Katie

ove myself? I come from a tough South Side Chicago neighborhood. We never learned about loving ourselves. We learned about how to numb our feelings with alcohol, and that felt pretty good. But love ourselves? No way. If a future Jenny had visited little Jenny in Chicago and told her that she was going to make loving herself her greatest mission when she got older, I would have thought for sure that meant that I was gonna either be a nun or turn into a giant dork. Obviously, the latter won out.

For years, everyone told me, "You can't love others without loving yourself." I pretended to understand and went through the motions but always felt like I was missing something—kind of like when Dennis Miller tells jokes and you laugh along with everyone else but secretly think to yourself, "WTF?" I suffered with this loving-myself dilemma for years in my twenties. I read book after book on how to love yourself, and I couldn't figure out for the life of me WHY this concept didn't hit home. Yogis would say, "Do you love yourself?" I would say, "I guess so. I'm not annoying to myself, so I guess I love myself." It seemed a little weird, but I still tried everything possible to accomplish this goal. I even tried hugging myself. I knew things got to be really dorky when I found myself doing affirmations in the mirror.

"I love you, Jenny . . . you stupid idiot."

I couldn't hold the seriousness of what I was trying to do for more than a few seconds at a time. It just seemed so lame, not to mention exhausting. I actually started hating myself for failing. Then I started reading books by Byron Katie, and my life was forever changed. I had to share her work with you in case any of you gals out there are also struggling to figure out how to love the most important person in your life . . . you!

JENNY: Byron, please tell everyone about "The Work" that you created to help people understand painful thoughts that we feel about ourselves sometimes.

KATIE: The Work is a way to identify and question the

thoughts that cause all the suffering in the world. It consists of four questions that you apply to a stressful thought. It's a way to understand what's hurting you, a way to end all your stress and suffering. It works for everyone with an open mind, and it has a profound effect on your whole life.

JENNY: It did mine! Talk about the four questions.

KATIE: The first question is, "Is it true?" The second is, "Can you absolutely know that it's true?" The third is, "How do you react—what happens—when you believe that thought?" The fourth is, "Who would you be without the thought?" Then you turn the original thought around, and find genuine, specific examples of how the turnaround is true in your life. This is a way of letting you experience the opposite of what you have been believing.

JENNY: How do you do The Work?

KATIE: There are detailed instructions on my Web site, www.thework.com. It's an amazingly simple and powerful process. The Work treats all stress and unhappiness at its source. When you question your thinking thoroughly, you return to your natural state of peace and joy, where depression, frustration, sadness, and anger can't exist. You become your own therapist, your own teacher, your own cure. There is no advice in The Work, no attempt at substituting positive for negative, nothing that you can do wrong, no goal. The only thing you need to bring to it is a willingness to answer the questions. It's not a process of learning; it's a process of unlearning. I found The Work— or more accurately, The Work found me—when I was extremely depressed and suicidal, and had been for ten years. One morning I opened my eyes, and all that darkness was gone. What I discovered in that moment was that all our suffering comes from believing our stressful thoughts. I saw that when I believed my thoughts, I suffered, but that when I questioned them, I didn't suffer, and I have discovered that this is true for every human being. We believe a stressful thought, and suffering follows. We believe, "He wronged me," for example, and the cycle starts. I suffer from believing that he wronged me, and then I try to place blame or guilt on him, and it cycles back and forth.

That's the power of an unquestioned thought. You can be in heaven and think, "That guy is playing his harp too loud," and the instant you believe it, you have kicked yourself out of the awareness of heaven. The difference between heaven and hell is believing a thought that is untrue for you. It's the only difference. Earth is actually heaven; our unquestioned thoughts about it can make it seem like hell.

JENNY: Describe self-love.

KATIE: You know what it's like being in love with someone. You think that he is the most wonderful person in the world, you admire him, respect him, adore everything about him, even his quirks and foibles, even what seem to other people his "flaws." Well, it's like that, except that the person you're in love with is you. You're in love with what can never leave you. It's a constant state. Your heart is always open, because your mind is open, and your mind is open because you don't truly believe anything you think. When you love what is, when you love whatever life happens to bring you, of course you love yourself. You realize that everyone is a reflection of your own thinking. If you're angry or sad or disappointed in yourself, you have to project that onto your partner or your parents or your boss, but if your heart is at peace, that peace fills the whole world. You can't help loving everyone, because you love the mind that perceives them. I love everything I think, so I love everything I see.

JENNY: Some people might think that what you're talking about is narcissism.

KATIE: Actually, it's the opposite of narcissism. It might seem like selfishness, but it's beyond self. What you're in love with is not your little ego, it's your true self, who you really are, without any concepts or stories about reality. Personalities don't love; they want something. Love doesn't seek anything. It's already complete. It doesn't want, doesn't need, has no shoulds (not even for the person's own good). So when I hear people say that they love someone and want to be loved in return, I know they're not talking about love. They're talking about something else.

When I walk into a room, I know that everyone in it loves me. I just don't expect them to realize it yet. Seeking love is how you lose the awareness of love. When you believe the thought that anyone should love you, that's where the pain begins. I often say, "If I had a prayer, it would be: 'God spare me from the desire for love, approval, or appreciation. Amen.' " To seek people's love and approval assumes that you aren't whole. But you can only lose the awareness of love, not the state. That is not an option, because love is what we all are. That's immovable. When you investigate your stressful thinking and your mind becomes clear, love pours into your life, and there's nothing you can do to stop it.

JENNY: How can we increase self-love?

KATIE: The only reason that people don't love themselves is that they're believing stressful thoughts about themselves. "I'm not good enough." "I'm too fat." "He doesn't really love me." "I should . . ." "I shouldn't . . ." "He should . . ." "He shouldn't . . ." And on and on. When you identify and question thoughts like these, you always come out of that inquiry as a kind, happier person. I don't know of another way.

JENNY: Can you be in a healthy relationship without discovering self-love first?

KATIE: The short answer is no. Romantic love is the story of how you need another person to complete you. It's an absolutely insane story. My experience is that I don't need anyone to complete me. As soon as I realize that, everyone completes me. The only relationship that is ever going to be meaningful is the relationship you have with yourself. When you love yourself, you love the person you're always with, the person you have woken up with and gone to bed with every day of your life. But unless you love yourself, you won't be comfortable with someone else, because they're going to challenge your belief system, and until you inquire, you've got to do war to defend it. So much for relationships. People make these unspoken contracts with each other and promise each other that they won't ever tamper with the other person's belief system, and of course, that's not possible. But when you come to the place where you don't want anything from your partner, it's like "Bingo! You just won the lottery!" If I want something from my partner, I need to take a look at my thinking. I already have everything. We all do.

JENNY: How do women heal themselves after coming out of a rough relationship?

KATIE: Judge your ex, on paper. Download a Judge-Your-Neighbor Worksheet from www.thework.com and fill it out with the harshest and pettiest and most childish judgments you can come up with. Fill out a dozen worksheets, a hundred worksheets, and thoroughly question the statements you write. Question everything you think about him. It works!

Once we begin to question our thoughts, our partners—alive, dead, or divorced—are always our greatest teachers. There's no mistake about the person you're with; he or she is the perfect teacher for you, whether or not the relationship works out, and once you enter inquiry, you come to see that clearly. There's never a mistake in the universe. So if your partner is angry, good. If there are things about him that you consider flaws, good, because these flaws are your own, you're projecting them, and you can write them down, inquire, and set yourself free. People go to India to find a guru, but you don't have to: you're living with one. Or you just broke up with one. Your partner will give you everything you need for your own freedom.

JENNY: How do you know when you're ready for the next relationship?

KATIE: You're ready for the next relationship when the next relationship appears, and not one moment sooner. How do you know that you're ready? There he is! How do you know that you're not ready? There's no one you're attracted to, or the men you're attracted to aren't interested. That's how it works.

JENNY: How do you not confuse feeling spiritually ready with just needing companionship?

KATIE: Well, sweetheart, the wonderful thing is that you can't make a mistake. If you're doing The Work on a daily basis, questioning your stressful thoughts about your ex or your father or mother or past lovers or boss or employees or children, you come to see whatever happens as good. Maybe a new relationship is premature, maybe not; maybe it will work out, maybe it won't. You look forward to it all, because you know that anything that happens is an opportunity for waking yourself up.

JENNY: What do you do when you're hurting from loneliness?

KATIE: I can find only three kinds of business in the universe: mine, yours, and God's. (For me, the word *God* means "reality." Reality is God, because it rules. Anything that's out of my control, your control, and everyone else's control—I call that God's business.) Much of our stress comes from mentally living out of our own business. When I think, *You should love me, you should be with me, you should do what I want,* I'm in your business. When I'm worried about earthquakes, floods, war, or when I will die, I'm in God's business. If I am mentally in your business or in God's business, the effect is separation. That's where loneliness comes from. It has nothing to do with whether you're with a partner or alone. You can't be lonely unless you abandon yourself.

JENNY: When a girl looks outside herself for love and gets fed love through her companion, why does it feel so good even though it's not the "correct" way to experience love?

KATIE: The ego loves being adored, even though it knows that what he is adoring is a facade. If I don't want to have sex when he wants sex and I pretend that I want it, he is attracted to the woman who wants sex right now, not to me. When he thinks of "me," it's the wrong one. When he rewards me and I feel what I interpret as his love, it isn't me he is loving, it is someone I was pretending to be. His affection has been bought with my inauthenticity. This may feel good for a while, but it is fragile and never lasts. It's not a question of the "correct" or "incorrect" way to experience love. What you're talking about is something other than love. Approval? Validation? Love is serene; it's fearless; it's complete. If you're looking to someone else to fill you, you can be sure that what you're looking for is something other than love. Nothing outside you can ever give you what you want.

7

Masturbation:

The Other Kind of Self-Love

hope no one who is reading this book is judgmental of those of us who masturbate. If you are, please burn this book in the nearest fireplace and say a prayer. For those of us who have experienced lust upon ourselves, let's get it on!

I went to Catholic school all my life. We had sex ed, but it consisted of a nun saying, "Don't have sex or you will burn in hell," and then showing us pictures of deformed genitals due to STDs. One gruesome deformity after another, which to this day I'm sure don't exist. I mean, how does a penis mutate into two penises? How can a vagina grow actual grocery-store-quality mushrooms? So gross. Maybe it was a doctored video the Catholic Church sends to all the schools. Anyway, it was disgusting and scared the crap out of every fifth-grader. I remember thinking that maybe I should become a nun so my odds of having a deformed vagina would be zero. But by the time puberty kicked into high gear, I threw away any thoughts of wearing a habit after Tom Kolajaczek gave me a hickey. The hormones that unleashed made me want to dry hump every altar boy that walked by. Then a miracle happened in my life, and his name was Tubby. Tubby was a stuffed bear that my mom bought me on sale at Kmart. Tubby accidentally got caught between my legs one night while I was trying to close my window and HELLO! Tubby set off an earthquake all over my body. I lay in bed, shocked. How did this bear that only cost $5.99 give me so much pleasure? I had heard about masturbation from my friends, and they talked about how disgusting it would be to touch yourself, so I avoided the idea like the plague. Then I thought, What if I'm not touching myself, but Tubby is?! Poor Tubby had no idea what he got himself into that night, helping me shut the window. The chubby polyester bear's new job lasted years. It was like he was working in a North Korean hard labor camp. I could swear the once-smiling bear actually lost his smile.

To me, Tubby was brilliant because I knew he didn't have an STD and I didn't have to feel guilty about getting off because I wasn't touching myself, Tubby was. Let him burn in hell for being bad, I was going to heaven. I was a senior when

Tubby and I ended our relationship. Not because I outgrew him or found a replacement; it was a forced separation. I came home from cheerleading practice one day and saw my mom having a YARD SALE! And someone snatched Tubby up!!! I was devastated and horrified at the same time. My Tubby was gone, and the thought of the poor jerk that actually bought a puberty-scented bear made me want to die. It wouldn't actually surprise me if I happen to turn on *Jerry Springer* one day and see Tubby telling his appalling tale of abuse.

I finally graduated to using myself to "release built-up pressure," but after a while, even I bored me. Luckily, I then discovered something called the pocket rocket. And listen to me, ladies, if you don't go online and order it right now, you are missing out on the most incredible orgasms of your life. If you think your husband will feel insecure about you getting a vibrator, then just be sneaky by giving it to him as a present and tell him you are going to "perform" for him. I'm not kidding you when I promise you will hunt me down and thank me for giving you the best experience of your life.

Some guys feel so threatened by a woman masturbating, like we prefer the vibrator to him. Well, the truth is . . . sometimes we do. The first of the two reasons I think we prefer to masturbate is that we enjoy not having to return the favor. We just want to get off and be done with it. The second reason is that we can orgasm when we want to. Sometimes we feel bad if our man is down there too long, so we end up faking an orgasm for fear that he might run out of air and die.

Besides the obvious enjoyment that comes from masturbating, I'd like to share with you the many health benefits associated with it. Some Web sites claim that women can build resistance to yeast infections, relieve chronic back pain, and help PMS and bad period cramps. (I just had to test out this last one, considering I get cramps like a sixteen-year-old girl. I usually fall into a fetal position one day a month and scream for hours. Sure enough, when Aunt Flow arrived, I crawled to my bedroom, grabbed the pocket rocket, and completed the mission. As soon as the orgasm had subsided, my cramps disappeared for a full hour. It freaking worked! Okay, so it was only an hour, but if you get cramps like I do, an hour is like heaven.)

There are also health benefits for men when they choke their chickens. It's a great form of stress release, improves sleep, is a mood booster, and cleans out their pipes, which helps lower the risk of prostate cancer, so say the Web sites. Maybe that information will help you women out there who are against your husband masturbating be a little more open to it. I've met many women who have a problem with it because it feels like they are being cheated on. A lot of guys use porn to get off when masturbating, so to the wives it seems like they are *lusting* after someone. I used to be like that in my twenties. Now when I'm not in the mood to have sex, I'm begging a guy to order *Big Honkers* on the pay-per-view porn channel.

Many cultures and religions frown upon the use of masturbation. They even label it as sinful. Throughout history they've convinced people that you could go blind and/or deaf, grow hair on the palms of your hands, get acne, and even burn in hell. Some went so far as to create contraptions for your genitals that had locks on them so you wouldn't touch yourself. In older dictionaries the definition for masturbation was self-abuse. Unbelievable. I also found the most amazing literature on steps to overcoming masturbation. It's not a joke. This is a Mormon "guide," circa 1970. It's called *Steps in Overcoming Masturbation* by Mark E. Petersen, Council of the Twelve Apostles. I was laughing my head off reading it. I don't mean to make fun of it, but the suggestions they offer to stop masturbating actually make me want to go masturbate. Check it out.

1. Never touch the intimate parts of your body except during normal toilet processes. Avoid being alone as much as possible. Find good company and stay in this company.

2. If you are associated with other persons having this same problem, you must break off their friendship. Never associate with other people having the same weakness. Don't suppose that two of you will quit together, you never will. You must get away from people of that kind. Just to be in their presence will keep your problem foremost in your mind. The problem must be taken out of your mind, for that is where it really exists. Your mind must be on to other and more wholesome things.

3. When you bathe, do not admire yourself in a mirror. Never stay in a bath more than five or six minutes. Just long enough to bathe and dry and dress, and then get out of the bathroom into a room where you will have some member of your family present.

4. When in bed, if that is where you have your problem for the most part, dress yourself for the night so securely that you cannot easily touch your private parts, so that it would be difficult and time consuming for you to remove those clothes. By the time you started to remove protective clothing you would have sufficiently controlled your thinking that the temptation would leave you.

5. Go into the kitchen and fix yourself a snack, even if it is in the middle of the night, and even if you are not hungry, and despite your fears of gaining weight. The purpose behind this suggestion is that you get your mind on something else. You are the subject of your thoughts, so to speak.

6. Never read pornographic material. Never read about your problem. Keep it out of mind. Remember—"First a thought, then an act." The thought pattern must be changed. You must not allow this problem to remain in your mind. When you accomplish that, you soon will be free of the act.

7. Put wholesome thoughts into your mind at all times. Read good books—church books—Scriptures—

Sermons of the Brethren. Make a daily habit of reading at least one chapter of Scripture, preferably from one of the four Gospels in the New Testament, or the Book of Mormon. Above anything else, the Bible can be helpful because of its uplifting qualities.

8. Pray. But when you pray, don't pray about this problem, for that will tend to keep it in your mind more than ever. Pray for faith, pray for understanding of the Scriptures, pray for the missionaries, the general authorities, your friends, your families, but keep the problem out of your mind by not mentioning it ever—not in conversations with others, not in your prayers. Keep it out of your mind!

Tried 'em all. Didn't work. I'm so gonna burn in hell.

To end this chapter, I thought I would show you some of the funniest names guys have come up with for their masturbation ceremony:

Unloading the gun, feeding the dog, milking the prostate, churning butter, dishonorable discharge, punching the clown, Uncle Gary's spray hour, beating the meat, polishing the Bishop, milking McNuggets, slapping the monkey, playing Yahtzee, throwing the dice, wrestling the one-eyed serpent, feeding the ducks, five against one, greasing the weasel, one gun salute, summoning the genie, varnishing the flagpole, whaling the dolphin, and my personal favorite . . . making sock babies.

8

If I Can't Have You . . . No One Will: Abusive Relationships

ost girls have dated one man in their lifetime who was jealous, controlling, or just a real jerk. I have successfully dated all three in my twenty-five years of dating. The friends I've talked to who have also dated these types of men now can spot them a mile away and run for the hills. But looking back into my

own past, I'm amazed that we allowed men to be anything other than respectful partners gliding through this game called life.

My first memory of getting ridiculed by a guy came in seventh grade. He used to punch me in the arm and then tell me I was an idiot with a face that only dogs could love. I used to go home and secretly cry because I had found some truth in it. I went back to school every day in fear I would get abused worse than I already had. So, what did I eventually do to prove my self-worth? I dated him. Yes, that's right, I dated him. I found that I wasn't the only idiot in the female race to date a man that is an abusive jerk. Looking back, I realized I wanted to prove to him I was worthy of his respect. I wanted to prove to him that I didn't have a face like a dog and that I could be pretty if he just really looked at me. Yes, this was only seventh-grade "love," but these moments are what usually set boundaries and goals for women later in life. My self-worth was then only measured by what other people would say to me. I would believe someone else's low opinions because they had to know best. I didn't know who I was, so I needed people to do that for me. This led to being involved in two destructive relationships that brought me down even further. The more I was controlled, the safer I felt. The more I was shit on, the more I felt driven to prove my love to someone. Yes, this is sick, but a majority of women are attracted to the bad guy. Hopefully most women will outgrow these types of relationships, but if they don't, the consequences could be deadly.

One of the most infamous murder cases involving a jealous and abusive husband was Dorothy Stratten. She was a beautiful young girl living in Canada when a creepy sleazebag named Paul Snider discovered her working in a Dairy Queen. He started dating her and took nude photos of her and sent them in to *Playboy*. She was accepted and became Playmate of the Year. Not passing up a golden ticket, Paul the sleazebag married her in Las Vegas in 1979. From what the stories say, he was so controlling he poisoned her dog because he was jealous of the attention Dorothy gave it. He also wouldn't let her drink coffee so she wouldn't stain her teeth. By 1980 Dorothy had gained some self-worth; she separated from the bastard and moved in with Peter Bogdanovich. Paul the sleazebag, obviously insane, then hired a detective to follow Dorothy. He also made a "sex bench," which was basically a chair with a built-in dildo, in the hope that he could sell it at a popular sex shop in Los Angeles and make millions off of it. (Fortunately, his invention was rejected.) Not long afterward, he asked Dorothy to meet them at their old apartment to try and hash things out. Dorothy agreed. (Obviously a dumb move, but haven't we all done the same thing just to get an ex to calm down?) She arrived with $1,000 in cash, hoping to settle the split and move on. When she arrived that afternoon, she was raped and then shot in the side of her face. The "sex bench" was also next to the bed, and according to police reports, it was set in a position for "possible rear entry intercourse."

On Dorothy's Playmate profile sheet that all Playmates fill out, she wrote that her turn-offs were jealous men. She should have listened to her instincts.

Ironically, as I write this chapter, Oprah is on TV, doing

a show about abusive relationships. She just stated that most murders happen after the wife gets out of the marriage. Weird, huh? Sometimes the ex-wife goes back to try to calm the monster or is forced to go back because of shared custody. The expert on the show, Gavin de Becker, talking about his book *The Gift of Fear*, said that you must have a plan and get help if you think your partner has the potential to be violent.

They say timing is everything; clearly I was meant to pass on credible advice by an author who knows what the hell he is talking about. So please check out de Becker's book if you're considering escaping from a bad relationship.

Because I don't want to just crap on crazy men, I'm also going to remind you of the infamous death of Phil Hartman, who lost his life at the hands of an abusive wife. Brynn Hartman married the lovable Phil Hartman in 1987. As a result of her failed modeling/acting career, Brynn's jealous outbursts wreaked havoc on their marriage. She eventually turned to drugs, which drove her into a deeper tailspin. Close friends said it was uncomfortable to be around them due to Brynn's mental state, and the more famous Phil became, the more psychotic Brynn turned. One night after a particularly brutal argument, Phil told her the marriage was over. Not surprisingly, this did not sit well with Brynn. On May 28, 1998, as he slept, Brynn, drunk and high on cocaine, put three bullets into her husband's body, ending his life. She then turned the gun on herself a few hours later.

People might think, Why didn't he get out sooner? My guess is there were kids involved. And like most people I talked to who have been in abusive relationships, there is a thing called hope they hold on to, thinking their partner might change.

The majority of my friends who have "good marriages" have said that their marriage involves typical fights but never anything that gets out of control. There are sincere apologies and efforts to improve themselves, and neither partner ever feels like the other disrespects them. But I've also talked to women who had been verbally abused and asked them to share some common insults their abusive partners would say on a regular basis. Here are just a few:

"You gonna wear that?"

"You look like sh*t."

"I don't want to have sex because you got fat."

"Why can't YOU dress like that?"

"You're stupid."

"You're sleeping with _____!"

"I'm glad you're not pretty."

"I so want to get on that [other hot chick]."

"You can't go out like that."

"Shut the f*ck up."

Obviously, since I'm not privy to the details of anyone's personal relationship, I can't give customized advice, or tell you to get the hell out of a specific relationship. BUT, I highly suggest that if anything in this chapter rings a bell, please go see a therapist to help decipher if the problems in your relationship merit counseling—or if you just need to get away from the asshole you're with.

9

Chocolate

Throughout my life I was a typical PMS chocolate eater, and then in my early thirties my true love for chocolate began. I found myself eating more and more chocolate every day. I don't mean just a candy bar here and there. I was up to about ten chocolate bars a day. I was embarrassed to let anyone see what I was doing, so I would hide and eat my chocolate in privacy. At night, I would hear the sounds of the gas station calling, telling me the different bars they had. When those voices won, I would load Evan in the car and drive to Mobil at eight o'clock at night just to sink my teeth into sweet Reese's Peanut Butter Cups, Kit Kats, Twix, Snickers, and Whatchamacallits. People would come over to visit and open a drawer to look for something, only to find foil wrappers exploding from it. My acne then became so bad I had hair extensions added to conceal my face. I even bought Proactiv because I wouldn't dare to give up chocolate for the sake of vanity.

Then Easter came along, and my body began to convulse with excitement. Chocolate bunnies, chocolate eggs, chocolate everything! I went to an Easter egg hunt with Evan and found myself at the children's table peeling off wrappers and shoving chocolate into my mouth with the five-year-olds. When we came home from the Easter party, Evan took a nap and I sat there poking through his Easter goodie bag. By the time he woke up, I had consumed everything in it. "Mom, what happened? What happened to my chocolate?" he asked in his cute, innocent voice. I replied, "Um . . . the Easter bunny came back over when you were asleep and said this chocolate was old and that we should go pick up new chocolate at the gas station." He looked at me strangely, but before he had time to comment, I threw him in the car and drove to the gas station. I felt horrible that it had come to this. What mother gorges on all of her son's chocolate on Easter from his basket? Something was wrong with me.

Later that month I had a meeting with my son's doctor, Dr. Jerry Kartzinel, who treats Evan's medical condition. I noticed that his eyes kept moving to my forehead and chin while I was talking to him. I said, "I know, my zits are out of control. I'm so embarrassed. I know you're looking at them." He said, "Jenny, you have to be loaded with candida." I replied, "No, Evan has candida." He said, "Darling, you do, too. Are you obsessed with chocolate?" I replied, "I'm not obsessed with it, I just want to actually marry a chocolate bar and make love to it and eat it for the rest of my life." He replied, "Honey, you have candida. Your zits and cravings will disappear if you trust me on this."

This is the same doctor who healed Evan, so I trusted that he was right. Now, let me explain candida for all those not in the autism world. Candida is a type of yeast. We all have it. The problem with it is only when it gets out of control. How does it get out of control, you ask? Well, after you take antibiotics, they strip all good and bad floras from your gut. We generally don't know to follow up the antibiotic with a probiotic (probiotics contain good bacteria, which help keep the gut healthy; natural probiotics can be found in yogurt). When good bacteria are not present, yeast grows rampant if the host consumes sugar. Then the host experiences mood swings, severe acne, rashes, bloating, chronic fatigue, and food allergies. In severe cases, people have all of those reactions, and I was one of the severe cases. I immediately went on 200 milligrams of Diflucan a day for sixty days, and I felt like the exorcist was being forced out of my body. I was angry, bitchy, exhausted, gassy, and just plain miserable. I wasn't allowed to eat sugar during this time. Candida dies when it's not being fed sugar, which was why I was experiencing those symptoms: that is what you feel like when those bastards are dying inside you.

By day 30, I noticed that my acne was not only gone, but I now had the most beautiful, glowing skin I had had in years. My moods had stabilized. By day 60 I had not one single craving for my old lover chocolate. To this day, I can actually hold a chocolate bar in my hand, and take it or leave it.

I thought it was important to tell this story in case other women out there are cheating on their husbands or boyfriends with chocolate. There are many reasons we love chocolate. It comes from the seeds of a tropical tree, and it is the most craved food in the world. We each eat almost 11.5 pounds annually. There is a whole list of substances found in chocolate too boring to run through, but the bottom line is that these substances trigger the release of mood-enhancing chemicals in the brain. Some researchers say that one particular substance releases dopamine in the pleasure centers of the brain, which peaks during orgasm. So no wonder we often prefer chocolate to sex.

Other researchers say that women crave chocolate during PMS because it contains magnesium, and that during PMS we actually have magnesium deficiency. Then there are the emotional chocolate eaters, who consider chocolate to be a sinful treat. When they are in a bad mood, it lifts them up and makes them feel like they are getting away with a little naughty treat.

I have experienced an amazing combination with sex and

chocolate. Not dripping it on body parts—that's just stupid, and it gets sticky. I'm talking about eating it while having sex. Go pick up some of your favorite chocolate (mine is chocolate-covered strawberries), and try it out. I shit you not, it's extraordinary. If sex is mostly a chore for you, then this can definitely make the task a little sweeter.

10

Dating the Teletubby

I dated this chubby, hairy guy named Eddie for a whole ten days. I thought a chubby, hairy guy would love me more because I was pretty and he was chubby and hairy. I remember looking into his eyes and thinking, Wow, I'm gonna get so loved by this guy. He's gonna make a great boyfriend/husband and will be so good with my future children because he's not the model type. Then I had sex with him. He had the skinniest penis I had ever seen. It was like a pencil. . . . No, a straw. Wait, those are the same size. Okay, it was a string. A hard string. Like an un-cooked piece of linguini. Yeah, that's it. It was a long, hard, uncooked piece of linguini. In my head I thought, Ew, what the hell am I supposed to do with this thing? Boil it and serve it for dinner? Then I thought, Wait, with this string/noodle he has for a penis, there is no way he's gonna cheat on me. And I'm prettier than anything he could ever get. He must be so insecure about his tiny dick that there is no way he's gonna hurt me or leave me . . . first. This guy is safe!

Now I didn't really have this conversation in my head. This was all done unconsciously, of course, but if you could press a button and play back what my unconscious could put into words, it would have sounded just like that.

We talked on the phone for hours, of course. New love, that's what you do! He would tell me sad stories about how his dad was always a total "Debbie Downer" in their relationship. He spoke of how hard that was on him, and I thought it was so sweet that he was revealing his past wounds to me. He finally invited me over to his house and I was taken aback by the disgustingness of it. It wasn't dirty, it was just pathetic. He lived in the basement of a shack. It wasn't even a house. It was a shack, AND he didn't even score the top floor. He was in the freaking basement of the shack. This would have been fine if he was in college or maybe his twenties, but he was thirty-nine. So now I find myself dating a fat, hairy, spaghetti-dicked thirty-nine-year-old man. (I was twenty-five.)

He then gave me a tour of his "crib," which consisted of me standing in the same spot and just spinning around. The basement was the size of a garage that could *maybe* squeeze in one and a half Toyotas. He had me lie down next to him, and when I plopped my body down I almost became paralyzed. My body was expecting a mattress, but all that was there was a pile of fifteen blankets all on top of each other—the bottom layer being cold concrete. It was like those dirty shacks that crazy loners live in, in movies that take place after nuclear war. I know what most of you are thinking right now . . . What the hell is wrong with her? Why is she dating this guy? Or if you are a fat, hairy man reading this, you're probably asking, "Hey, how can I get me some of that?"

As I lay there running my hands over his hairy man boobs, the smell of mold was starting to asphyxiate me. I just kept thinking, How does this guy not have brain damage from all this mold? He asked me to spend the night, and I said okay— but I lay there on the floor of his basement trying to breathe into a Kleenex, hoping it would block black mold spores from entering my lungs. Needless to say, I didn't sleep much that night—mostly because of the raccoon family that lived in the wall next to the bed. I bet their place wasn't as bad as this. But I also lay in this shithole trying to convince myself that this guy was the one. Seriously, this is right after I did *Singled Out.* I'm still young, cute, and have a little career. What the hell was wrong with me to think that this was what I deserved? I would rather live in a shitty basement with this Teletubby than ever give myself a chance at real love. The next morning I surprised him by telling him I was going to treat him to a romantic night at the Four Seasons in mold-free luxury. He seemed excited.

So that night in the Four Seasons we had sex, which felt more like a Pap smear, and then fell asleep watching some stupid movie. The morning after, I thought I would surprise him with a beautiful breakfast hiding in the other room. He woke up and entered the living room to find me smiling next to a table of food. "Good morning!" I said. He looked at the food, picked up a bagel, and said, "What the f*ck is this?" I was speechless. Did he just say, "What the f*ck is this?" Yeah, I'm pretty sure he did. I thought maybe he was joking around with me, so I responded, "It's my bunion I just cut off my foot." He said, "I don't eat f*cking bagels," and threw the bagel down on the table.

Yes, that's right. The Teletubby just yelled at me and threw the bagel on the table after a night of sex in luxury. I could understand if it was bacon and he worked for PETA or something, but it was a freakin' bagel. Again, I sat there in shock and felt a huge wave of anger rush through my body. I stood up, walked slowly over to the door, opened it, and calmly said, "Get the hell out of here." He grabbed his shoes and walked out the door. That was the last time I ever saw Teletubby.

Now, let's dive into the psychology of this, okay? I convinced myself that a chubby, hairy guy with no penis would make a really good boyfriend because he would never cheat on me and would worship the ground I walked on. If you think that is soooooo crazy and shallow, stop and look at the hot chicks in Hollywood who date the ugliest rockers. I mean, some of them make me want to vomit. I was no better! I was willing to sacrifice ever finding someone attractive, productive, sweet, with a nice penis and a home, just so the odds would be better that he wouldn't cheat on me or leave me. How pathetic. I sat alone in that hotel room forcing myself to ask these questions about myself. Am I that insecure? Why did I think I deserved a homeless Teletubby? I'm not saying all chubby, hairy men that sleep on concrete are losers; I'm just saying, Aim higher. The answers I found were that my ego felt safe with him, and I also felt more powerful in that relationship because I was the one with an actual mattress. His ego probably couldn't handle the fact that I had running water. I wasn't trying to flash money, but I was thinking that maybe he would love me more because I could treat him to nice things. I felt like I had nothing to offer personally because I felt worthless and unlovable. Amazing, but true.

I don't know why we all have to go through the "I'm worthless, I'm not worthy" stage in our lives. I think some never wake up to it. They stay in abusive relationships. I've met so many amazing women in my life who have shocked me when they introduce their boyfriends, who are total losers. I want to shake them and tell them how much better they deserve, but I guess we all have to find our own way to that secure enough place of "I'm lovable, I'm worthwhile, and I deserve heaven." I obviously managed to get past homeless guys, but now I'm requesting heaven in every relationship I have. There is nothing more important to me right now than making sure the friends I make and the men I make out with are a reflection of my new happy self.

11

Couples Counseling

Therapy rocks. Seriously! I think if couples therapy were a requirement, the divorce rate wouldn't be nearly as messed up as it is now. I sat down with my own therapist, Elizabeth Halliday-Bluestone, to interview her on ways to help make relationships work. (Because based on my current status, I'm clearly in no position to tell you how to make your relationship work. Elizabeth is much more qualified.)

JENNY: You had told me once that when people first come in for couples counseling, many times it is too late. Why is that?

ELIZABETH: Based on my observation, most couples seem to seek help when their relationship is at its worst. Whether it includes issues that range from emotional or physical abuse that could include extramarital affairs, or a myriad of other problems, the damage is already so profound that Dr. Freud himself would have a tough time seeing them through to a satisfactory resolution.

JENNY: So when should couples start counseling?

ELIZABETH: Couples who are smart come in when they recognize that there are issues in their relationships that are already causing difficulties between them. If they can recognize that there are problems early on, the anger and resentment that has been building up between them is much easier for the therapist to work with. In my experience the couples that do want to get their relationship back on track before toxicity can really set in have a much better chance of working through their problems while in therapy. For example, a wife would be able to say honestly to her husband, "You know, working so late at night is something that really bothers me, and I have an issue with it. I need to talk to you about it because it is upsetting to me." At this point the resentment and anger can be dealt with in a much more productive manner.

This is because their individual feelings about each other have not yet created a situation where their issue cannot be discussed in an effective and positive way. The resentment and anger is much less.

JENNY: Do you notice couples coming in that don't want to try and work on anything and just want you to help them to break them up?

ELIZABETH: Yes. In my practice I have found that many couples come in and have no desire to even try to work on the presenting issues. Many times they simply would like to figure out how to get out of their relationship gracefully, especially if there are children involved. They would rather let a neutral party negotiate the separation.

JENNY: Do you think they also come to you to figure out the actual reasons why they're breaking up, so they have an understanding of why this is ending?

ELIZABETH: Absolutely, many couples have a need to know why their relationship has crumbled. However, they are also looking for validation that the end of their relationship was their partner's fault and not entirely theirs.

JENNY: What is one of the hardest issues for couples to get through?

ELIZABETH: Without a doubt, infidelity is the hardest issue for couples to resolve. It is very difficult for the one partner to trust someone after his or her significant other has had an affair. However, when some of my patients have only had an affair that lasted a very short time, their odds in making their relationship work increases significantly. It's still incredibly difficult emotionally, but not as hard as an affair that has been going on for an extended period of time.

JENNY: Why is it that each person's perception of the same situation is so completely different? Are men really from Mars?

ELIZABETH: Yes. Men are from Mars and women are from Venus. This is because men, honestly, communicate in a totally different fashion than females.

JENNY: How do they, if you can explain it?

ELIZABETH: I believe that females are intuitive, emotive, and more sensitive to their world and universe. We are by nature predisposed to being caretakers; it is in our female DNA to be more nurturing and caring when faced with different challenges. If we look back to the time of cavemen, we find that the men's main responsibility was to provide the food and clothing for their tribes. Their task was to hunt and club down bison to use their hides for warmth during the winter months. In contrast the women stayed close to their caves and taught their children the basics of language and social skills. As primitive as that may have been, their roles were starting to be clearly defined. Clearly things have come a long way since the time of cavemen, and we all know that men are taking on more and more responsibility in the home and emotional caretaking of their children. I think men have really stepped up to the plate beautifully, but today, the majority of the caretaking is still done by women. And we, as women, want to talk to our partners. At the end of the day we want to talk about our day's activities and how we are feeling. Men do not always want to participate in this kind of conversation. We tend to be the talkers! Feeling that we have not gotten our emotional needs met, we start to feel angry and resentful. We have a need to say, "I want to go to this deeper level, and I want to have you share these conversations with me, and I want to know how you are feeling also." This is not most men's natural inclination. You can almost hear them saying, "Boy do I want to watch the basketball game!" Men's thinking tends to be much more linear and black and white. While most men are willing to address issues that arise in daily life, they usually become very uncomfortable with women's need to explore every facet of their emotional decisions. For example, we would like to know what you are feeling, what you are thinking about, and how we fit into that. Many men don't even think about it. In fact they are surprised when their women say they are not getting what they need emotionally. Sometimes they've never even thought about it. They just think differently. So my job as a therapist is to get the two planets, Mars and Venus, to communicate with one another.

JENNY: Well, then teach us how!

ELIZABETH: Okay. One of the most important aspects is to build up a toolbox of communication skills that includes learning how to speak to one another, learning how to listen, and, most significantly, to be compassionate and understanding of your partner's feelings even if you do not agree with them. Without these tools, what occurs in the relationship is interpreted by the other as anger, criticism, resentment, and hurt. That's a recipe for disaster. First and foremost, the couple will never be able to listen to each other because the attacks are so aggressive. I would say no one would want to stay and listen to that. They are not going to hear a thing, and they're not going to respond in any way, shape, or form except, "Go to hell! I'm out of here!" As opposed to talking through the issue in a way that both partners can hear—*what* I call the "honey before the vinegar" technique.

JENNY: I *love* "the honey before the vinegar." Please explain it to the ladies.

ELIZABETH: The key to success with this technique is to be able to start your sentences with "I" statements rather than "You" statements. For example, "*You* always do everything wrong—this is *your* fault." Let's just say a woman would like to go out with her friends on a

Wednesday night for dinner and a movie. If her partner becomes angry and unreasonable about her activities when she goes out, a productive way to express herself might go like this: "When I go out on Wednesday night with my friends, it makes me feel happy and connected to another type of world. It is not that I don't want to be with you tonight. I love you. It's just that I would like a little break from our daily routine now and then. So I would really like to understand why it makes you upset, because that is not my intention."

Now that is honey and vinegar, because you are telling your partner the truth in a calm and loving way without saying something as dysfunctional as "You're a controlling jerk that never lets me do anything!" That is simply stirring the vinegar.

JENNY: Can you say, "I felt angry about it . . . ?"

ELIZABETH: You know what, I don't believe in anger, Jenny. I just don't. I've told you that underneath anger is always a feeling of abandonment, hurt, and powerlessness. Anger is in my opinion a defense mechanism that keeps us from dealing with our real feelings. It's always hurt that's underneath anger. Anger and denial are as vulnerable as a small scab that one could scrape off only to find numerous untreated emotional infections. I like to stay away from the A-word. I don't believe in it.

JENNY: So "I'm hurt" is a better way of saying it?

ELIZABETH: Yes, that's the truth. If my husband came home and was angry with me, I would want to know why and talk about it. Years ago I probably would have shut down completely and given him the silent treatment for a few days. I would like to think I've grown a bit in my twenty-five years of marriage and that I practice what I preach. I am also incredibly lucky to have a husband who is not an intrinsically angry person. But there are many occasions where we are emotionally in very different places, and I do get frustrated. So then I pull out my toolbox.

JENNY: I shut down. I totally shut down. I sometimes shut down for three years after one anger burst from a partner.

ELIZABETH: Yes, I'm your therapist. (Laughs.) I know!

JENNY: What are the stats today for divorce?

ELIZABETH: Today, one out of two marriages in America wind up in divorce.

JENNY: What?!! That's not good. Why is it so bad?

ELIZABETH: It really is quite a disturbing statistic!!! Now, let's combine that with all the unresolved issues that people have not dealt with from their past childhoods, and you have the perfect recipe for disaster!!!!! There are two sets of baggage people have to deal with. One from their pain of childhood that they have never quite come to terms with, and another set of baggage whose tag reads "Adult." They are one and the same! And of course I use that word loosely. The couples with the best chance to have a successful outcome in therapy are the ones who recognize there are problems early on in the relationship. They come to see how their childhood defenses can create all the fighting and dysfunction, and *then* they start to build their toolboxes based on their new knowledge of themselves.

JENNY: Okay, give us another tool.

ELIZABETH: The time-out tool.

JENNY: I *love* the time-out tool.

ELIZABETH: I know you do!

JENNY: Just to fill people in, my ex-husband John would follow me around the house arguing with me, and instead of ever coming to a resolution, he would just go back to the beginning of the problem and repeat it all over again. It was like he was on a hamster wheel. That's what I used to call it when he would take me all the way back to the beginning of the problem after I thought we had resolved it. So I would run from room to room telling him to shut up because we were getting nowhere.

ELIZABETH: Yes, so when you came in, I told you that either party gets to call a time-out when you feel like both of you are getting too heated and the situation is not getting resolved. The length of the time-out can be decided by the couple. Those can vary from couple to couple. But the most important aspect of this tool is to revisit the same issue after having thought it through in a quieter atmosphere. I also suggest that to go past one half hour is too long. The goal in this technique is for cooler and calmer heads to prevail while thinking about a more positive resolution to the problem.

JENNY: Mine was ten minutes. And it absolutely saved my life. I had moments of peace throughout the day when I got to call the time-out.

ELIZABETH: Yes, but I want to emphasize that you are *both* in time-outs. Not just one of you. Couples need to know it's a two-way street, and during that time you're not supposed to zone out. You are working alone on how to resolve the situation. Then after ten minutes or however long you choose, you come back together and hopefully utilize the honey and vinegar technique. One of the best lines I can give to a couple to start off with after an unsuccessful time-out is always "I am still confused." Hopefully their toolbox is full enough to get through the existing problem.

JENNY: That is a good one! It takes the power or charge out of the fight.

ELIZABETH: Absolutely. It's not an attacking phrase like "I'm angry at you. I hate you. What you are saying is stupid and ridiculous." So by saying, "I'm confused," you have changed the dance step. When two people are doing the same dance of dysfunction, like a tango, nothing changes. If the other person has gone to therapy on his or her own and has come to much self-realization, the dance step will change. This person may have learned a new dance step like the waltz. So what does that other partner have to do? He or she will need to figure out how to do the new dance, and may in fact stumble for a while. Whoever is the one doing the right functional dance will use their communication tools to help their partner learn how to participate together as a team. Always of course using the honey and vinegar technique.

JENNY: So now we've got what sounds like two good tools. "I versus You," and then we've got the time-outs. What about compromising?

ELIZABETH: Compromising is incredibly important, and a huge tool for the toolbox. There has to be compromise, or there is no relationship. It has to be an accepted compromise on both sides. If you are not willing to compromise, you are going to go straight to divorce court. I promise. Compromise is key to any relationship.

JENNY: So you don't necessarily defend something that you feel is not a big deal? Like if my future guy wanted me to text on my phone less often.

ELIZABETH: That's fine as long as he compromises in return. It must be a two-way street—otherwise you just feel controlled and manipulated.

JENNY: Wow, that's a really good point. So if I compromise to text less, I could tell him in return I want more cuddle time after work?

ELIZABETH: Absolutely. And by the way, if you are with a guy where *you* have to compromise your need for cuddling, in my opinion you're with the wrong guy!

JENNY: Which brings me to my last question: "Can I bring my next boyfriend to you before I get serious with him?"

ELIZABETH: If you don't I'm gonna crack your . . . head open.

JENNY: I'm serious.

ELIZABETH: So am I!

12

The Power of a Loving No

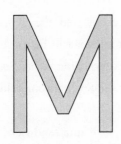y entire life, I have been doing things I don't want to do for the sake of helping others and winning their approval. I endured years of grooming by nuns to pretend that I cared what people were talking about; to act as if I enjoyed people I couldn't stand; and to do things for people when they asked me to, even though I didn't want to. This kind of conditioning has caused me so much misery. Some might read this and say, "Of course you should do those things, you selfish brat. Those are all acts of kindness." But are they? Do acts of kindness

require one person to be miserable to make another person happy? It just doesn't seem right. I had to learn my lesson the hard way and have only become awakened to this at the age of thirty-seven. I'm hoping this chapter can teach you the power of a loving no, so that you too can save years of discomfort. So now I would invite you to open your mind and think back to all those times you did favors for people, had sex when you didn't feel like it, and stayed friends with someone way past the friendship's expiration date—and learn the importance of making yourself happy.

As far back as kindergarten my teacher told the class, "Saying yes to people when they ask for a favor will help you make a lot of friends," in her chipper brainwashing voice. So, with that in mind, I was the girl that did whatever anyone told me to do.

"Jenny, go smash that bug and then put it in a sandwich." Okay. "Jenny, can you do my homework for me?" Okay. "Jenny, listen to the priest and smile when he tells you the story of Jesus for the next five hours." Okay. "Jenny, go steal a fifth of Bacardi from the store." Okay. "Jenny, can you work on Christmas Day for the fifth year in a row?" Okay. "Jenny, will you give up all your friends because I'm your boyfriend and you don't need them anymore?" Okay. "Jenny, can I borrow two thousand dollars?" Okay. "Jenny, can you skip your sister's party tomorrow and help me move my furniture into a new apartment?" Okay.

Relationships between husbands and wives can sound a lot like this. The husband is usually asking the questions: "Can we please have sex even though you don't want to?" Okay. "Can we watch hockey instead of the season finale of *Dancing with the Stars*?" Okay. "Can you let my parents come on vacation with us?" Okay. "Can I go out with my buddies this weekend even though you've been locked up in the house with the kids all week?" Okay. "Can we spend the money on a flat-screen TV instead of your new boobs?" Okay.

I know there are some tough women out there who will be reading that last bit thinking, "No way, I would kick his ass. Over my dead body would I ever let him get away with that." Well, then I would say to read that last paragraph again with you being the one asking the questions, and your husband always saying "Okay." Maybe he's miserable, and you don't even know it. The thing that I want to make clear is that I'm not saying you can't agree to compromise and truly help someone out when they need it. What I'm saying is that you have to truly *want* to do it. Only if you *want* to do it, you say yes. If you don't want to do something, the response is a loving no. I have found that people can connect to the honesty and not hold hostility when it's an honest no.

Usually, most people who are able to do this were raised within a family that encouraged them to speak their mind. My best friend in Chicago was raised in a family that taught her to speak up about everything, and have debates at every dinner because their parents read that's what the Kennedys did. If my friend's dad caught her saying yes to something she didn't want to do, he would shout, "I know you don't want to do that, tell the person no. Stand up for yourself." So my BFF Julie went on to grow up into a telling-you-what-she-thinks-all-the-time kinda girl. I became friends with her twenty years ago and was drawn to this quality I never had. She was the one that would tell guys to "leave Jenny alone" because I couldn't tell the guy no. She would pick up the phone and make me call my boyfriend on spring break and tell him the truth about being at a party and not a movie. I was raised to lie to protect people's feelings, and to be submissive and surrender my opinion so other people felt good about themselves. Doing otherwise is still something I have a hard time with, but every day I practice to get better at it.

But back to Julie. Even though she carried the ability to say no so easily, she lost many jobs as a result of speaking her mind. Julie had to learn something called an "open mind" that her father didn't teach her when debating at the kitchen table. She was taught that you find an opinion, you stick to it, and you fight for it. Her relationships were suffering because she was as unbalanced as me, but in the other direction. She's in couples therapy right now, learning that when you win an argument, it doesn't always mean you were right.

Julie pointed out something about me the other day that made me go "Hmmmmm." She said, "I think because you have been so submissive your whole life, I don't think you know who the hell you are." I was stunned for a second, but realized that Julie was just telling it like it is. She was right. I have been so much the "okay" and "yes" girl that I have a hard time giving my opinions on things. I always learned to go with whatever the majority says. I would even borrow opinions from friends and boyfriends about who I should like best on *American Idol*.

My most recent experiment with an honest no happened only this past spring. I went to my friend Chelsea's book party and while I was there, I saw Cloris Leachman waving me over. I walked over to her table, and she shouted, "I just wanted to meet you." I responded with, "Thanks, it's really nice to meet you, too." She said, "I need to have your phone number." I stood there for a long uncomfortable twenty seconds and responded with a sweet smile and the word "No." Normally I would have said, "Okay," as usual, but why the heck would I give her my number? I don't know her, and it was awkward. She responded with, "Well, I just want it." For most of you who watched her on *Dancing with the Stars*, I think you will agree that she was a real hoot on that show . . . but not someone you want calling you at night to shoot the shit. I had to muster up the strength to say kindly, "Well, I don't like giving my number out, but it was really nice meeting you," and then I walked away. I was so proud of myself for being able to give a loving no, and Cloris seemed fine with my final answer. (She very well could have flipped me the bird behind my back, of course, but what you don't know can't hurt you.)

Anyway, for all you "yes, okay, sure, I don't mind," people out there, I hope this chapter will give you a little insight to just try an honest no. See how it feels. It might do your relationships—and your health—a lot of good.

13

Breaking Up: How Do You Know When It's Over?

t's impossible to write this chapter without correlating it to my last relationship. So I plan on interviewing people on why they broke up and how they knew it was over. Sorry, I won't kiss and tell about my last relationship, but my friends will spill the beans on theirs. . . .

My friend Kim had been married to a man for six years. She had a child with him and for the most part was head-over-heels at the beginning of the relationship. Then the phone calls began, with her bitching and moaning about how annoying he was. I decided to sit down with her to ask how she knew it was over.

JENNY: Bitch, what happened to your marriage?

KIM: (*Laughs.*) Looking back at my relationship, I have to say that I stayed in the relationship two years too long.

JENNY: Did you try counseling?

KIM: Yes, but there was so much resentment toward each other that the odds were not good. The damage was too deep. We tried to see each other's perspective, but it got to the point where we were just not able to move past our grievances.

JENNY: You said that you stayed in the relationship two years too long. What was happening two years ago that started to give you signals that the relationship was on its way out?

KIM: Um . . . well . . . I couldn't stand the way he chewed his food, and when he would touch me, my skin would crawl. We never kissed anymore, not that I wanted to— he was lazy and would not help me with the baby, which made me hate him even more.

JENNY: If this were going on for the last two years, why would you stay in it?

KIM: Fear of being on my own. I have a kid and was a stay-at-home mom. We barely made ends meet together, and the idea of splitting up half of nothing terrified me.

JENNY: So . . . then obviously something must have happened where your happiness became more important than your bank account.

KIM: You know, I started reading books that opened my mind into thinking that things might actually be okay if I chose happiness. All those "everything happens for a reason" and "everything happens for the best reason possible" books made me take a chance.

JENNY: So when you told Mike you wanted a divorce, what happened?

KIM: He lost his shit and threatened to get custody of the child. I laughed at him because he doesn't even know our pediatrician's name or the brand of chicken nuggets our child likes. I told him we could share custody, but I'm out and that's it.

JENNY: So did he leave or you leave?

KIM: He left and I stayed in the house until we sold it and split the money. Then I asked my mom to move out from Iowa and help me with my kid so I could get a job. I started teaching yoga again, which I love to do more than anything in the world, and recently I just got an offer to open up my own studio.

JENNY: Do you look back now and think, "Holy shit, I did it"?

KIM: Yes, and I don't want to act like it was all peaches and cream after the split. It was hard, and I felt very alone at times, but I trusted that good things were ahead and kept my thoughts there.

JENNY: Watching you go through this was tough. The majority of women I asked who were still in miserable marriages wouldn't leave out of fear of money and their kids. You're a really good example of trusting your instincts and having faith in a better outcome. I love ya, bitch.

KIM: Well, if you really love me you'll do a yoga DVD with me someday.

JENNY: I'd rather do a beer-chugging DVD. I'm much better at it.

———

To be fair, I hunted a guy down to get his perspective on how he knew his relationship was over. His name is Kevin (no, it's not, but I have to use a fake name). Kevin wasn't married, but he'd been in a relationship for seven years and recently called it quits. He is a friend of a friend of a friend, so his story was new to me, too.

JENNY: I hate that you're hot.

KEVIN: Why?

JENNY: Because I'm gonna want to make out with you.

Kevin looked at me strangely, not getting my humor.

JENNY: I'm kidding. (I kinda wasn't.) So, tell me what happened in your relationship and how you decided it was over.

KEVIN: It wasn't fun anymore. It was as simple as that. I realized you can come up with a zillion reasons why things went bad, but the easiest thing to realize is that if you're not having fun in life, change your life.

JENNY: So . . . did you dump her?

KEVIN: We both knew it was over. The fights became so bad. She was moody and wouldn't let me do what I wanted to do.

(Wow, I was totally digging this guy's point of view. So guy-ish.)

JENNY: Out of curiosity, what didn't she let you do?

KEVIN: She would bitch at me when I wanted to hang with my friends, but after working all week I needed some guy time. Then she started getting careless about sex and whined more than talked.

JENNY: What made you stay in it for seven years?

KEVIN: Well, it really only got bad in the last four years.

JENNY: What made you stay in a shitty relationship for four more years?

KEVIN: I kept thinking it might change. And so many people bitched about their relationships, so I thought it was normal.

JENNY: Then what made you say, No more?

KEVIN: I wanted to feel happy again, and together we were miserable. I also thought about my life and that I'm thirty-seven, and never pictured myself to be as miserable as I was. I think all you have to do is ask yourself that question, "Am I happy?"

JENNY: Again, just out of curiosity, not trying to probe [yes, I am] . . . do you blame her for your unhappiness?

KEVIN: Um . . . Well, I know I was a prick sometimes, too. But she did most of the complaining.

JENNY: But I bet you were really great at ignoring.

KEVIN: How did you know that?

JENNY: (*Laughs.*) Well, if one person does all the complaining, the other one usually has to do the ignoring.

KEVIN: Yeah, I guess you're right.

JENNY: So what lesson did you learn out of this?

KEVIN: Don't stay in something so long if you're miserable.

JENNY: As I'm sure you know, I am no longer in a relationship. In ending it, I learned that if I blame any partner for my unhappiness in the relationship, I lose the lesson from it. Do you feel you could look inward and see that everything had to do with you?

KEVIN: Um, no.

JENNY: Okay, well then, let me bring up when you said, "She got careless about sex." That's true?

KEVIN: Yep.

JENNY: Can you put an "I" in place of the "she" and repeat it back to me?

KEVIN: I . . . got careless about sex?

JENNY: Yep. Name three reasons why that's true.

KEVIN: (*Sitting there, dumbfounded.*) Um . . . I wouldn't go down on her anymore cuz she annoyed me.

JENNY: That sounds careless to me. Two more . . .

KEVIN: She would only get horny when she ovulated, and I wouldn't have sex with her to piss her off and to make her see what it felt like when I wanted sex and she said no.

JENNY: That sounds pretty careless to me. One more . . .

KEVIN: Why are you doing this to me?

JENNY: Sorry, it's just the tools I used from Byron Katie at www.thework.com, and I think it will be helpful for the book. You're doing well. Just one more. You can do it.

KEVIN: Um . . . [*Thinking now while two minutes pass.*] I don't know if I want the next one in the book.

JENNY: Well, then, I won't put it in the book. [*Hahaha.*]

KEVIN: I would hold off coming just to make her work extra hard.

JENNY: Great job! [*Asshole.*] Now you can see that you were calling her what you found in yourself. So go make a list of everything that's wrong with her and turn it around on yourself.

KEVIN: That sucks.

JENNY: It totally sucks, but it's totally true. It's amazing how much resentment and anger leaves once you do it, though.

I said good-bye to "Kevin," and I'm sure he thought I was an asshole, but what I was saying is true. If I looked to blame my partner, I lost all the wonderful lessons my teachers (ex-boyfriends) reflected back to me. I think the message we can all take away from this is that the universe will only move you toward the direction of happiness if you listen to your emotions. And trust that everything that happens is for the best reason possible, even if it is saying good-bye to someone you deeply loved.

Part Two

LUST . . . .

14

Fantasies:
Our Secret Life

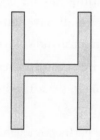ave you ever planned a vacation or a big girls' night out, and months before you had visions of how much fun it was going to be? You saw you and your friends dancing on the dance floor, shoving cheeseburgers in your face at four in the morning, and then puking everything up the next day. Then days before your big trip, you call your friends, saying, "It's gonna rock!" because in your head it was already the best time ever! Then cut to the actual

trip . . . and the hotel is under construction, you can't get into any clubs, and your friend is on antibiotics so you have no one to drink with. The obvious point being, your fantasies are pretty much *always* better than the actual event.

Getting older, I've had to learn this lesson the hard way. Sometimes fantasies are better off staying fantasies. As soon as we try to play something out in real life, our expectations of them are so high because we are counting on the end result to match the fantasy to perfection. Sexual fantasies are usually the biggest disappointments to play out. Why is that? I think it's because they are so incredibly erotic in our imagination. There are no consequences, no guilt, no insecurities, when you're imagining having sex with other people in your head. I'm sure we all have fantasized about having sex with one of our husband's/boyfriend's friends, and it totally got us off. But then having to actually go through with it would result in devastating consequences.

But why the need for fantasies? Aren't our partners enough? Can't we look at them and picture having sex with *only* them for the REST OF OUR LIVES? Ummm. I don't think so.

In my "expert" opinion, fantasies help increase arousal and desire for more sex. My favorite foreplay is not having my boobs squeezed or even oral sex. It's dirty fantasy talk. That's how I can get in the mood. *Then* you're welcome to squeeze my boob or go down on me. I think a lot of that has to do with women today being so busy: our minds are usually stuck on what groceries we need rather than sex. We need mental stimulation to divert us.

So is fantasizing actually a bad thing? Does it hurt the relationship? Some Web sites claim the reason people fantasize is that they are secretly unhappy in the relationship, or their spouse is not giving them what they need. I don't know what eunuch wrote that, but I think it's bull.

One fascinating aspect of fantasies is that they are so secretive. One of my favorite things to do is uncover things that people just don't talk about, and fantasies make the top of the list. Go ahead and ask someone what he or she fantasizes about. The look on their face goes from embarrassment to changing the subject. We don't even feel comfortable talking about our fantasies with our best friends. Why is that?

I think we are fearful that our friends will think we are too perverse. I mean, I know I come up with some pretty crazy scenarios, so I'm sure most of you do, too. But if you're a schoolteacher, how do you tell your friend that you dream about the science teacher molesting you in the nurse's room at the school? You don't. You keep that in your secret dirty world. It's even hard for me to tell any man about some of the twisted scenarios that I conjure up in my head. Sometimes I think, Jeez, Jenny, get a grip.

I surveyed both girls and guys on my Twitter account (which is @JennyMcCarthy) about what their most common fantasies were. I was amazed to hear what all of you girls had to say . . .

Doing Strangers

This isn't really one of my favorites because, let's face it, it's more fun to imagine somebody we know cuz it's naughtier. Even in romance novels they don't say, "A stranger walked in and made mad passionate love to me." It's usually something much more perverse like the woman's cousin she had been longing for her entire childhood. Don't get me wrong; there have been many "faceless men" in my fantasies. But it had more to do with the scenario, like being tied up, than it had to do with a stranger walking in and having sex with me in the middle of the night. Strangers, just on their own, don't really ring my bell.

Rape

Now here's where a stranger could actually be useful. I have no idea why women even fantasize about this, but many have. This is one fantasy, of course, you never want to have played out, but for some reason being forced to have sex is on the top of the naughty-naughty list for girls. If your man ever tries to play it out, it can come across as cheesy. "I'm here to rape you now, okay?" Just doesn't seem like actual rapist talk. But if you want him to be a little more aggressive so your rape scenario works in your head, just tell him to throw you around the room and rip your clothes off. This is definitely a fantasy that you *have* to be in the mood for, otherwise you might punch your partner in the face. And that's another fantasy altogether.

Orgy

The word *orgy* entered the English language in 1589, but orgies have been going on long before there was a name for them. Orgies were actually "normal" back in the old days. I shouldn't use the word "normal," I should say, "more accepted in society." People would throw parties with alcohol, sacrifice an animal, and then they would all roll around in the bushes getting it on. The hippies brought "free love" back into society and made orgies a popular extracurricular activity again in the 1960s. The problem is, they also brought a rampant outbreak of STDs, not to mention out-of-control pubes and armpit hair. The only issue I have with the word *orgy* is that it immediately makes me think of the nude camps from those *Real Sex* episodes on HBO, the ones that show nudists with the ugliest, creepiest bodies you've ever seen. (Women who are seventy and have zucchini boobs hanging down to their toes should never be in an orgy, or at least not one that's on TV.) Anyway, I think most people at one point have fantasized about rolling among a group of naked people. It's erotic to think of limbs surrounding you, not knowing who you are kissing or who's kissing you.

But as you get older, I highly suggest keeping your zucchinis to yourself and your partner.

Doctor

Playing doctor was common in our childhood. Well, at least it was in mine. We would show our butts or flash our tops. All pretty innocent, but it's still intriguing to me that we were turned on by examinations even at an early age. The most obvious sexual fantasy one would think you would choose would be your ob/gyn's office. But most of our ob/gyns aren't attractive in the least bit. Think about it. A guy who had to get a degree just so he could see a woman's canooter is probably not that cute. Sometimes you can forgive balding and big bellies for the sake of the fantasy. I found myself fantasizing the "replacement" ob/gyn taking over for my chubby one, who called in sick. There is something incredibly arousing about being examined. Let me rephrase that. There is something incredibly arousing about *fantasizing* about being examined—because in *real* ob/gyn visits, KY Jelly and a Pap smear metal vagina opener don't really turn me on.

Being on Display

Come on! Who has not fantasized about being a stripper or even a hooker at one point? It's funny how incredibly judgmental we are about these two professions, yet in our fantasies we are the star stripper and the naughtiest whore in the brothel. Being on display and having men lust over our bodies is incredibly arousing. For example, performing in the middle of a room at a bachelor party or sliding down a pole at a strip club while having guys slide money in your G-string is hot. We want to be drooled over. We want guys to have that look on their face like we are meat and they are starving. In reality, though, our partners don't necessarily go to that hungry place like we need them to. So, we fantasize it. It's usually, "Hey, babe, are we doing it tonight?" when sometimes we just need to hear, "Take your clothes off, you naughty slut, and spread your legs." We might just do what they want—for a really big tip, of course!

Girls, Girls, and Some More Girls

Listen, ladies, I was blown away by all the responses I read about girls fantasizing about other girls. Almost every woman, according to my Twitter poll, said that they had at least one fantasy about being with a woman. Maybe men are supposed to be extinct someday, and we're just preparing ourselves.

Two Guys

Yes, why wouldn't we want another guy to get busy on us? Usually this is where you are having sex with your partner and his friend comes into the room. That seems to be the most typical for the "two guys at once" scenario for girls. Unless your man's friend looks like Mr. Potato Head, then just picture Brad Pitt.

Strap One On and Dominate Your Man

I can honestly admit I have not entertained this fantasy . . . yet. And I'm sure any guy I'm with would be grateful that I don't feel the need to attack/have at his butt with my fake penis. But to all those chicks out there that do, God bless you! Seriously, I read that it has to do with wanting to feel in control, and many women don't normally in marriages; so they go to fantasy world, where they can make their guy bend over and take a butt beating. Wow. Fantasies can be so entertaining!

I'm sure women have many, many more fantasies; these were just the most common in my poll. What I also found fascinating is the fact that most women have fantasies while having intercourse, whereas men are in the act and concentrating on what's in front of them. (At least according to my Twitter respondents.) It's a whole different ball game when it comes to masturbation. I think masturbation is 95 percent fantasy-driven for both sexes. But when it came to sex, I was shocked to see how many guys said, "I'm mainly just focusing on my wife the majority of the time." They followed it up, of course, by saying, "with the occasional 'my wife making out with a chick in the bed,' but mostly just my woman." I think that has to do with them having to do most of the work during intercourse. They have to concentrate, while we get to close our eyes and imagine having sex with their best friends. Hahaha.

15

Sexual Harassment

Being blond with fake boobs in Hollywood, I have experienced many different forms of sexual harassment. Some would argue that I deserve it for being blond and implanted with saline. To some extent, yes. I know that if I were to wear a tight shirt one day and happened to walk past a construction site, I would hear, "Nice knockers." I don't want to hear that, but if you are going to attempt to look hot, catcalls are inescapable.

The casting couch is a whole other story. It's not only real, it's actually happening right now in many offices in

Hollywood. A girl who just moved into town is currently at some cheesy audition for a movie and is being asked to take her clothes off. How do I know this? Because I've lived in this business for seventeen years. Oh my God, I just counted on my fingers how long I've been trucking away in this business, and it really is seventeen years! Ugh.

Anyway, when I came off the bus from Chicago, someone immediately approached me on the street to do postcards for Hawaii. I was so excited by the idea of doing something with my clothes on, because *Playboy* was the last thing I did back in Chicago. I guess it didn't matter I wasn't Hawaiian or a hula dancer, but I thought if they don't care, I don't care. I received an address and was told there would be a hair and makeup person so I didn't need to come camera-ready.

This was my first major photo shoot outside of *Playboy*, and I called my mom from the car. "Mom, Mom, I'm already working out here! I'm on my way to a photo shoot to do postcards for Hawaii." Mom replied, "Oh, Jenny, I'm so proud of you. I'm so glad that you get to take pictures with your clothes on!"

I hung up and pulled down an alley and saw the address on the back of a garage. I parked my car and walked over to the door. The garage itself looked like it was about to fall over and as if it belonged to a serial killer. I did what most girls do when they come to Hollywood: I ignored my instinct and knocked on the door. "Come in," said a scary, grizzly, serial killer voice. My stomach knotted up, and I pushed the dilapidated door open. Inside it looked like Satan's dojo. I felt a trickle of pee come out of me and didn't know whether I should run or say something. Around the corner the grizzly voice showed his face. It was the scariest Hell's Angel I had ever seen. (I could only compare to Hell's Angels in movies, and this guy looked like the prototype.)

"Go over to my girlfriend, she's going to do your makeup." I looked to the right, and there was a drugged-out, scary-looking truck driver of a woman sitting on the ground. I knew that if I ran away at this point, I would be murdered. I forced a smile to try to calm my nerves, and slowly walked over to her. "Come sit down on the ground here. I can't get up right now, I hurt my back," she said. I didn't think her back was hurt at all. I think she was so high she couldn't stand. She pulled a used powder puff out of her purse and started wiping my face with it. "I forgot mascara, but you don't need any." Oh my God, Oh my God, Oh my God, was all I kept thinking to myself. The Hell's Angel/serial killer photographer came over to me and said, "Your outfit is on the set."

Set? Did he just say set? We were in a garage with swastikas and pictures of naked women with demon heads hanging on the walls. "Okay," I quivered. The drugged-up "makeup artist" mumbled, "Your hair is fine, go." I got up and walked toward a backdrop of a Hawaiian sunset with a surfboard on the ground. Next to it was a bikini bottom and a Hawaiian lei. "Um, are there any coconut cups to use for the bra?" I gently asked.

"No," he grumbled. I walked behind the backdrop of the Hawaiian sunset shaking in fear of what this guy was capable of doing to me. He actually had a camera and a light box, so I thought that was at least a good sign that he was intending to take a picture and not just rape and kill me. I put on the bikini bottom and put the lei over my naked breasts. This is not what I had in mind, but again, I was afraid for my life so I just was going to do what he wanted me to do and go. I came around the backdrop, and he said, "Lie sideways on the surfboard." So I held the lei on my chest so it wouldn't reveal my nipples and slowly lowered myself to the floor. "Okay, look sexy."

He snapped a few pictures and then said, "Okay, now get rid of the Hawaiian lei." "*What?!*" I replied. Oh no! He's going to rape me now. I stood up and started stammering, "Um . . . um . . . listen . . . um . . ." And then I heard my instinct say, "Tell him you are under *Playboy*'s contract, and that if you pose nude we both will get sued." So I repeated what was in my head, and he started screaming, "That's f*cking bullshit!" then proceeded to throw shit around the room. "Just take your clothes off, and I'll hold these pictures for a year." The argument continued . . .

"But I just thought we were doing Hawaiian postcards?"

"Don't be such a bitch, just do it."

"Can we just reschedule to do nudes tomorrow, so I can at least shave and look hot?"

"You look hot now."

I didn't know what to do, so I walked behind the backdrop and quickly got dressed, but shouted out that I was taking my clothes off and I would be right there. As soon as my last piece of clothing was on, I bolted out the door and ran to my car. I didn't know what a Hell's Angel dude was capable of, so I drove as fast as I could out of there. Needless to say, I never went to a shoot again if I didn't know what I was getting into.

Many years later, after I became famous, I was in Hawaii with my boyfriend and I went to a drugstore, and there I was on a Hawaiian postcard, lying on a surfboard. I couldn't believe it. I had never been paid for that job, and my manager (who I was dating) was furious. I tried to tell him that it didn't matter because the man would probably try to kill me. He thought I was being overly dramatic and decided to call the postcard company to track down the photographer. Surprisingly, he did. The phone conversation went pretty much like this:

MANAGER: Hi, I represent Jenny McCarthy. There were photos taken of her three years ago that you sold to a postcard company without paying her.

HELL'S ANGEL PHOTOGRAPHER: If you ever call me or contact me again, I will hunt you down, go to your office, and shoot you and then shoot everyone in your office.

Needless to say, my manager thought it was a good idea to let this one go.

Even later in my career, with agent and manager representation, I continued to be sexually harassed, sexually groped, jumped on, and asked to remove my clothes during auditions.

I took a vow to myself when I came out to L.A. from Chicago that I would never sleep with someone or get naked for a job. Mind you, for a great pair of shoes I might give a hand job with lotion, but for an acting gig? No way. The reason my acting career never really panned out was probably largely due to me not putting out to get ahead. Whatever. I'm happy where I am now, and probably saved myself from many STDs.

16

STDs: The Gift That Keeps on Giving

O kay, so I did some research to prep myself on these love wounds, and I'm so incredibly grossed out by the pictures I found. You are so lucky I'm not doing a pop-up book on STDs, because you would sew up your canooter after what I just allowed myself to see. It felt like sex-ed class all over again.

STDs have been around for hundreds of years. Some really smart historians believe that syphilis was brought to Europe by Christopher Columbus's sailors on their return from the New World. I was shocked when I read that. What in the hell were they poking around in? Many people believed that the early stages of syphilis were the beginning symptoms of gonorrhea. Then this British surgeon named John Hunter wanted to verify that there was only one infection, so he injected his penis with material from a patient with gonorrhea. I know! Gross! When he developed the signs of syphilis he determined that syphilis and gonorrhea were indeed the same infection. However what the lunatic didn't take into account was that many suffered both infections at the same time. So Christopher Columbus's sailors brought back two gifts from the New World, not just one. It was a French doctor in the middle of the nineteenth century who convincingly demonstrated that it really was two separate infections. I wonder what he put into his penis to finally figure that one out?

Then in 1450 pubic wigs were created. Yes, that's right. I said pubic wigs. They are called merkins and were created initially to combat pubic lice. Prostitutes would also wear them to cover up signs of disease, such as syphilis. Jeez, can you imagine lifting up that pubic wig and finding that kind of surprise? I thought my blown-out vagina from childbirth was bad. Merkins are now used for actors to cover up their meat and potatoes during the filming of love scenes. If you ever get a moment please go online and check out merkins. They are hilarious looking. I'm almost tempted to come out with my own line of them.

In the 1960s birth control became available, along with the

slogan "Make love, not war," and hippies had sex with pretty much everyone. I'm surprised their genitals didn't fall off. STDs skyrocketed, and because of antibiotics most people thought they were curable and no longer a health threat. This type of "free love" behavior ended abruptly when the public first became aware of AIDS. That was my puberty generation. My hormones were raging when all over the news, AIDS turned sex into a deadly activity. It was hard to get my brain wrapped around that. Of course my small gang of high school friends would say, "It's only for gay people, nothing is gonna happen to us." This kind of ignorant philosophy got many people in trouble. Luckily, I only dated Tony in high school.

Then I went to college down in southern Illinois. I know what you're thinking, do people actually live in southern Illinois? No, crabs do. Tons of pubic crabs took up residence on the campus when I went to Southern Illinois University. Looking back now, I don't understand why everyone didn't just shave their pubes, but I guess that really wasn't in style until the mid-1990s. I was so grossed out and fearful to be with any man that I basically would only let them get to third base with me. Even my roommate, a short, spray-tanned blonde named Missy, got crabs; I almost died when she told me that her crotch kept itching.

"I don't know what the hell is wrong with my crotch," she said.

"Well, maybe you have yeasty beasties."

"No, it's not inside my vagina."

"Maybe you have a rash of some sort or need a serious shower."

"I dunno. Let me go look."

A few moments later I heard a bloodcurdling scream. I thought a murderer had just entered our apartment, so I did what any good friend would do: I ran the opposite direction to save my own life. Screw her, I kept thinking. I don't like her anyway. As I was opening the back door, I heard her scream, "Jenny, look what just came off my vagina!" Oh, no, I thought. She's got crabs. I should still run for my life! She's infected. GROSS!!!

"Jenny, oh my God, please come here!"

"Dammit, Missy, I don't want to get fucking crabs."

"Please just come. Please!"

I ran to the kitchen and pulled out a Hefty garbage bag and opened it. I pushed both of my feet through the bag, wearing it like a diaper. Then I grabbed another one and wrapped my hair up in it like you would with a towel.

"I'm coming. I'm coming."

I entered the bathroom, and she started crying when she saw me. "What the hell are you wearing?!"

"Bitch, if I wanted crabs I would have gone to Red Lobster."

She started laughing, then I started laughing, and then she pointed to the dot on the counter.

"Look, it really does look like a crab."

"What the hell, Missy?! Do something before it freaking makes babies on the sink or something." She grabbed the phone and started dialing.

"Who are you calling?" I asked. Before she had time to respond to me, she said, "Hi, Mom," into the phone. Who in the hell calls their mom to tell them they have crabs?

"Mom. I have crabs."

Well, that's being direct. I could hear her mom shouting, "Oh my God, Missy. How many boys have you been sleeping with down there?" She responded with, "Everyone has crabs down here." To defend my cleanliness, I screamed, "I don't! I don't have crabs." My roommate looked at me and said, "I wore those sweatpants you're wearing last night to bed." Everything went into slow motion as I imagined the worst possible infestation colony of crabs bouncing from one pube to another. I saw them having orgies and being so happy that I'm half Polish because of the enormous amount of pubic hair I have. I finally snapped out of it and found myself tackling my roommate to the ground while wearing a Hefty garbage bag diaper.

"You bitch!" I shouted as I rolled my body on top of hers. She started screaming, "I'm just kidding, Jenny, I'm kidding! I didn't wear them. I'm just messing with you!" I stood up, pissed off and grossed out. My roommate grabbed the phone and continued her conversation with her mom and learned how to remove pubic lice with shampoo. I wore my Hefty bag underwear until we washed everything in the house thoroughly, and I made my roommate sleep on the kitchen tile floor for a week. We were one of the only apartments that was crab-free the rest of the year.

By the time I got to Hollywood, herpes was the new gross

"love wound" on the scene. I met a guy out here, who I slept with for six months. We were watching a herpes commercial on TV, and he casually said, "Oh, I have that sometimes." I slowly turned toward him and threw him a right hook. I only hit his arm, but I definitely bruised it. *"What?! You prick. You tell me six months later?"*

"I thought everyone had herpes, baby," he replied.

"No, I just moved out from Chicago, we only had to worry about crabs. You should have told me the first time. You totally could have given it to me."

"We never did it when I had an outbreak."

"Didn't . . . did you hear the commercial? You can spread it without having a breakout."

"Well, none of my other girlfriends got it from me."

I broke up with him. Not because of herpes. I could love someone with herpes. I was just upset by the fact he didn't care enough about me to tell me ahead of time. It's gotta be an uncomfortable thing to do when you meet someone new and you're hot and heavy and don't want to interrupt them with, "My cauliflower herpes don't seem to be there right now, let's have sex." Not the best kinda foreplay talk.

The moral is: be careful out there, ladies. One in four girls has herpes today! Like the saying goes, "Herpes is the gift that keeps on giving." And if you're not smart, you might have to get yourself a merkin.

17

Threesomes

I think at some point almost everyone has at least fantasized about doing a threesome. Then there are those who have done them and those who are willing to try it out for the sake of experimentation. I'll come right out and say that on *Howard Stern* I openly admitted to enjoying a threesome. I was a Playmate, and shit just happens when people are always naked.

One thing I have noticed is that the younger generations seem to be much more open to threesomes. When I asked girls in their twenties if they had tried it, the majority of them said yes. Mind you, this is L.A. When I asked girls in their thirties, half said yes, the other half said no. When I asked girls in their forties, only about one-eighth said yes. So if each generation is obviously becoming more open to multiple people in the bedroom, what does the future look like? If we evolve as time goes on, are we supposed to be a little more lax about monogamy? I wonder about it all the time. All you have to do is watch *Animal Planet* to see the dominant male lion sleeping with all his lion bitches. Or you can just switch the channel and see Jesse James and Tiger Woods doing the same thing.

But what do we do about this growing interest, to ask another canooter to join us in the bedroom? Do we open our minds and see what it's like, or do we close the door on the possibility of experimenting? I reached out to Patti Stanger, who stars in the hit Bravo TV show *Millionaire Matchmaker*, to help me out on this topic. She is very successful at hooking people up, and has heard just about every request from men around the world. I sat down with her at the Polo Lounge in Beverly Hills to discuss threesomes, next to a table of fifteen Kennedys celebrating a birthday. Just for shits and giggles, I purposely talked extra loud.

JENNY: How often do you hear about couples wanting to have threesomes?

PATTI: Well, I hear the clients coming to me, especially the men, "I want you to screen for breast implants and bisexuality, and I'd like to do threesomes."

And I say, "Look, I'm not Heidi Fleiss, that's not written on my head. I'm not going to jail for you, buddy. You want to do it, you have to do it with two consensual adults—and I wouldn't exactly approach it right away in the beginning of the dating stages. You gotta feel it out; after you've had, you know, sexual intercourse and you're monogamous, and then you bring the other party in. But be clear! If she's on the cusp and bisexual, she could leave you, because I see more women leave for the woman than stay with the man.

JENNY: What?!

PATTI: You heard me.

JENNY: Really?!

PATTI: Yes.

JENNY: Okay, so the girl ends up having another relationship with the girl?

PATTI: Because there's an emotional connection. And if you open that can of worms, be prepared to eat it, is what I like to say. Also another danger can occur when the man leaves the wife for the third party. One of my closest friends got a trainer because she wanted to work out. She and the female trainer really started to bond. She decided to bring her trainer home as a birthday present for her husband, and they did a threesome. He wound up leaving her for the trainer!

JENNY: What?!

PATTI: He left her for the trainer, and she got pregnant. The trainer got pregnant! Gets better. Then the jerk had another threesome and he left the trainer for the other girl in the threesome.

JENNY: What a man whore!

PATTI: It can obviously get out of hand. Couples need to be careful.

JENNY: You said this was a birthday present to her man. Are threesomes a popular birthday present?

PATTI: Yes. That's the time of the year. That's the birthday present. It's usually the five-year-, seven-year-itch marriage time, when you're not getting your kicks anymore.

JENNY: How common is it for threesomes to go bad?

PATTI: It's common. I have another friend of mine, I can't say who that person is, and I said to him, "What's the reason you got divorced from your wife? You were married to her for thirteen years." And he says to me, "We got too crazy sexual." Now this is a very good-looking sexual guy. . . . It turns out they were doing threesomes and it became an addiction. Then there's no intimacy between the two parties. It could become like, "That's our Friday night date." And then Saturday you're like, "Okay, what's next?"

JENNY: Trying to top it.

PATTI: It's like you start with pot, then you end up on cocaine, then you're on crystal meth, you know, living on the streets.

JENNY: But what do you do, or tell a couple, or give advice to somebody that has a bit of a stale relationship who says, "Maybe this could help us get over a hump?"

PATTI: A sexual therapist.

JENNY: Really? What would a sexual therapist do?

PATTI: There are certified sexual therapists that actually get in the room. You have to research this online, you have to make sure they are accredited, and they will get in the room and direct you two.

JENNY: No! But isn't that creepy?

PATTI: After a couple glasses of wine, you don't care. Because a lot of women are not climaxing during intercourse, because it's only 30 percent of the population that does . . .

JENNY: Seventeen percent.

PATTI: Now it's down to 17 percent?

JENNY: Yes.

So then how can a sexual therapist teach you to spice things up?

PATTI: So I think what happens is, you bring this therapist in the room, and you guys can really have the Kama Sutra, the kundalini, awakened. Remember, the kundalini can only be awakened at the serpent chakra when you're in love. You can't just do it for sexual gratification. So you want to get someone who's pretty open-minded and well versed in basic psychiatry skills; as far as, you know, marriage-family counseling, and knows all the medications, because some people are on meds and that's why they can't climax. And sometimes they get naked. And sometimes they bring in their partners to show how it's done.

JENNY: Shut up! Who gets naked?

PATTI: The best thing is the *Better Sex* videos.

JENNY: No wait, back up. Do the couples get naked?

PATTI: They could, and have, from what I've heard. But people could also get videos to watch and learn ways of spicing things up. The *Better Sex* videos are the best thing on the market.

JENNY: Okay, but does this look like the *Real Sex* series, where they all have like zucchini tits?

PATTI: No, these are good-looking people.

JENNY: So are you open to couples watching porn?

PATTI: Yes, porn is fine. Because you're going to lose interest. You can only stay sexually attracted for so long. My mother says it eventually dies, so you have to have humor and you have to have an emotional connection and then you've got it all. And if you can be sexually satisfied and have those three things you probably won't leave . . . doesn't matter if Brad Pitt falls from the sky, you're not gonna leave.

JENNY: I have a Brad Pitt story later in the book.

PATTI: Did you have sex with him?

JENNY: You're gonna have to read the book to find out.

PATTI: Bitch.

JENNY: So let's just say, by chance, people reading this still want to try out a threesome.

PATTI: You can try a threesome. There are rules, though, that would help make it not end in a disaster.

JENNY: Like what?

PATTI: Go to Vegas. Buy it. Get a professional. She cannot get emotionally attached. Get a clean professional in one of the cathouses that have been prescreened by a doctor. Now the reverse is harder, two men and a woman.

JENNY: So the majority of women haven't had two men and a woman?

PATTI: Straight men don't wanna cross swords.

JENNY: That's right, they don't, do they?

PATTI: No, they're afraid that they're going to be considered "gay." And that's the hardest thing for a man to do.

JENNY: That's kinda not fair. Don't you think that if we allow a girl in the bedroom, we should also be allowed a guy?

PATTI: What usually happens is the husband says, "What about if we do two couples?" And now you're swinging. So that's how you cross the street to swinging.

JENNY: That's the gateway.

PATTI: That's the gateway!

JENNY: And then you're on HBO's *Real Sex* sucking on zucchini tits.

PATTI: Exactly.

18

Fetishes:
The Need to Get Kinky

y friend Kelly worked as a paramedic and she said she loved her job because there was always something different each day. I could barely handle having my period every month, so I'm always amazed by the ability paramedics have to not vomit on their patients. Anyway, she was telling me a story about a call she and her partner answered. The 911 operator told them the man wouldn't say what was wrong with him. He just said

he needed help. They tried knocking on his door, and he shouted, "Please break the door down and come in." So Kelly and her partner tried kicking the door down and couldn't. She shouted, "Sir, we can't break the door down. We are going to call in the fire department to break it down."

"No! Please don't!" the man exclaimed. Kelly replied, "Can you tell me what's wrong with you, sir? Are you hurt?"

"I have a situation here, and I can't move."

"Well, the fire department is on their way." From that point on all they heard from the man was profanities.

BOOM BANG!

The firemen broke the door down, and they rushed inside the apartment. They found the man lying on the floor, naked, with a large frozen fish sticking out of his ass. They all stood there, shocked, just staring at this guy, who was lying on his stomach crying. The firemen were holding back laughter. Kelly said to the man, "What's your name, sir?"

"Mike."

"Okay, Mike. Did someone do this to you?" she asked.

"No, I get off by sticking things up my butt. I put the frozen fish up there, and it started to dethaw in my ass, so when I tried pulling it out, the scales started ripping my anus." (For all those who saw my movie *Dirty Love*, I put this in a scene.)

The entire fire department let out a gasp. Kelly got on her knees and started to examine his ripped anus. She knew there was nothing she could do without causing more tearing and pain. "We're gonna have to take you to the hospital, Mike."

"No! For the love of God. I can't be seen like this. I'm an executive." They put Mike on a sheet so he could remain on his stomach and then lifted him onto the gurney. The frozen fish was sticking out of his butt by four inches. It was just the tail end of the fish sticking out, and they were so grateful the fish was dead. They wheeled him through the elevator, into the ambulance, and then into the emergency room, where she had to tell the doctors about Mike's fishy fetish. They knocked him out, lubed his butt, and removed the fish. Since then, Kelly said, there have been a couple of other different types of fetish calls from all types of people, but nothing as entertaining as the "bass in the ass."

Sexual fetishes are defined as a sexual attraction to objects or material not normally considered sexual. They are considered healthy if you don't get stuck obsessing on them. One should also not kill anything, like a fish, hamster, or human. The majority of men I have talked to seem to have a foot fetish. I dated a guy once who would only reach orgasm during sex by turning around and looking at my feet. I would always get annoyed because I went through so much hell to get my boobs done, and the guy would only look at my feet. I even tried to keep them ugly in hopes he would look at my face during sex at least once, but no such luck. Feet were his boobs.

According to my Twitter poll, the majority of women liked their hair pulled. Hair pulling is more of a pain fetish, and I am guilty of enjoying the occasional pull myself. The problem is that most guys don't realize it's mostly about the timing of the hair pull and not the pull itself. The perfect time is once we start really getting into it and might reach orgasm, not the first thing on the list. Also pulling too hard, to the point that your partner feels like her head is going to snap off, is not a good thing. There were a few times I nearly punched boyfriends in the head for almost decapitating me.

I thought I would end this chapter by enlightening you with some interesting/disturbing fetishes that I have turned up in my research. Not only are these things real, they actually have freaking names:

Hybristophilia: Sexual relations with a convicted criminal. (I always wondered who those women were that married guys on death row. They're hybristophiliacs!)

Formicophilia: In which seeing insects crawling on the genitals leads to sexual arousal. (They should just get crabs, and their life would be complete.)

Autagonistophilia: Unlike exhibitionism, during which the person intentionally exposes their genitals to an unsuspecting stranger, in this paraphilia the person creates situations in which other people can see them in the nude, like leaving the curtains open and walking around the house naked in hopes that someone will peep in the windows. It is the thought that someone may be watching that is sexually arousing.

(Uh-oh, when I'm staying in a hotel room in New York and the next building is within sight, I think I'm an autagonistophiliac.)

Autassassinophilia: The person is sexually aroused by situations in which they may be killed. They have to feel they are in true danger in order to be sexually aroused. Unfortunately, some of them get killed in the process.

Mixophilia: The person likes to watch themselves or their partner engage in sexual activity. Usually this means watching themselves in a mirror (guilty as charged).

Infantilism: Dressing as an infant and acting the role of a child under two years old is sexually arousing. Including the hiring of a nurse or nanny to take care of you. (I shudder to think of changing *that* diaper.)

Symphorilia: Natural disasters are sexually arousing.

Catheterophilia: The person is sexually aroused by the insertion of a catheter.

Zoophilia: The person wants to be treated like an animal, wearing a collar and even eating out of an animal's dish. This is different from bestiality, which involves actual sex with an animal.

Coprophilia: Smearing human feces on yourself or having one smear it on you, causing sexual arousal. (Sorry, I had to put this in there. I just found this fascinating that there are so many people who do this that they had to name it something.)

Coprophagia: Eating human feces. And you thought smearing it on yourself was bad? I'm not making this shit up. Hahahaha. Seriously, this crap is real. Hahahahaha, gross.

19

What Happens

in Vegas . . .

DO NOT stay in Vegas . . . if you're famous. Celebrities used to think it was a safe haven for going to a strip club, taking home a stripper, and then playing Twister with her. Thanks to a hurting economy, even strippers are spilling the beans for big money to reveal their steamy nights with Mr. Famous. With the evolution of cell phones allowing normal folk to capture their dirty deeds, paparazzi no longer need to be omnipresent. All it takes is one click of a cell phone to have enough evidence to rat out a celeb. In doing so, I'm sure the snitchers give that money to charity . . . not.

I recently talked to a casino owner in Vegas and asked him why there weren't more paparazzi in Vegas. He told me, "Because we'd shoot 'em." He went on to say they try to protect everyone who comes to Vegas. Not just celebs but executives and anyone looking for a good time. He could have saved that whole sentence by just saying, "We protect cheaters the best we can." Sin City has always had the legacy of fulfilling our naughtiest desires and helping us let go of pressures from everyday life. But lives can be seriously destroyed in this town. People who don't even know each other get married in dinky chapels and then quickly try to annul the marriage after the drugs wear off.

Bachelor parties are the most dangerous events a dude can go to in Vegas, if he is attempting to be a monogamist. It's really hard for guys not to partake in some sort of raunchy business when girls are shoving cucumbers up their vaginas and asking dudes to insert a twenty-dollar bill in their sphincter. I've heard so many stories over the years and even crashed a bachelor party once to watch what went on. Let me tell ya, it didn't go too well for the bride. Every guy slept with or got eaten alive by the stripper. It made me ask the question, does this happen at the majority of bachelor parties? I was also intrigued by Nevada's brothels. If I was a horny dude looking for a Twister partner, a brothel is where I would go, only because of the strict STD screenings they do.

My curiosity on this particular subject was overwhelming, so I hopped on a Southwest flight and flew my ass to Las Vegas to interview girls at the number-one brothel in Nevada, the Chicken Ranch.

Walking into the establishment, I was really taken aback by how peaceful and quaint it was. The picture in my mind was taken straight from the movies. I pictured drunken people and naked chicks walking around. It wasn't like that at all. I opened the door and was politely greeted and told to go to a back bungalow, where I would get a chance to interview two working girls.

JENNY: Hey, girls.

ASHLEY: Hi.

MICHELLE: Hello.

JENNY: You're both totally hot. Like HOT hot.

ASHLEY: (*Laughs.*)

MICHELLE: What did you expect?

JENNY: Honestly, I wasn't sure. The only image of a brothel I had in my head were ones I had seen in movies, and the girls weren't that great looking. But you two are gorgeous! I should know better than to think movies depict real life. So do you gals *only* work here, or do you venture out, like a pizza delivery service?

ASHLEY: No, we only work here. When I was asking around about where to work, my friends all said, "Go work at the Chicken Ranch." I've been here for many, many years now, and it really is the best place.

JENNY: So let me fill you in on why I'm here. It's certainly not for the chicken. Wahahaha.

MICHELLE: (*Giggles.*)

JENNY: I'm here because I want a "look inside" as to what the hell happens in Vegas when our men go to bachelor parties or on an extended business trip. Do you think our men come here as naughty little bastards, or does Vegas make them naughty?

ASHLEY: Hmm, good question. I think that the guy is naughty already, and Vegas allows him to bring it all to the surface.

MICHELLE: It's Sin City. The potential to be naughty is at their fingertips. Especially when these guys are stuck in the same routine every day.

JENNY: Did you mean to say they are stuck in the same vagina every day?

ASHLEY: (*Laughs.*)

MICHELLE: (*Laughs.*)

JENNY: Speaking of needing variety, what percentage of married men do you see coming in?

ASHLEY: I probably see about 90 percent.

JENNY: *Oh my God.* That's a pretty big number. Do they come in bitching about their wives?

MICHELLE: A lot of times when they come in they just want someone to listen to them, so you tend to be the shrink.

JENNY: Really? Is that true?

ASHLEY: Yes. Sometimes they just want someone to feel compassion for them. To listen to their "woe is me" tale.

JENNY: Then I would charge them for my ear to listen to that shit.

ASHLEY: Oh, we do.

JENNY: (*Laughs.*) What about bachelor parties? Do you see guys coming in here for bachelor parties?

MICHELLE: We do. Quite a few.

JENNY: Do they cheat?

ASHLEY: Uh, yeah. Especially if they are coming here.

JENNY: Yeah, I guess that was a dumb question. Do you think men in general are just wired to have to have different canooters? Because in the animal kingdom you see the animals mating with their whole tribe!

ASHLEY: I think it's both men and women.

JENNY: Are they both getting action here?

MICHELLE: Sometimes. Not too long ago, women weren't even allowed in here; now they come in a lot. Some pick out who their husband should be with and then just drink at the bar and wait for him. And then there are other couples that want a threesome.

JENNY: The married men that come here to see you girls, do they want to leave their wives or just come in to taste the different flavors?

ASHLEY: They don't wanna leave their wives, they just want something different, and hence that's why we're here. There's no strings attached, we don't call them the next day . . . it's f*ck me, pay me, leave. That's it.

JENNY: What about little virgins that come in here?

MICHELLE: We get a few of those. I actually cater to a lot of first-timers . . .

JENNY: I would totally be into the virgins.

ASHLEY: A lot of them are thirty-year-old virgins.

JENNY: Oh . . . uh, on second thought . . . no I wouldn't. (*Laughs.*)

MICHELLE: I still enjoy them because they want to know so many different things. "What turns a woman on? How do I do this?" And they are so eager to learn, whereas a lot of guys are kind of set in their ways. "I'm just gonna do this, and I *know* it feels good to you." And we go, "Oh yeah baby, it feels great." But with a virgin you can say, "You know, women like this. Try to do this with the lady that you find."

JENNY: Do you ever get success follow-up stories?

ASHLEY: Yes! I constantly get e-mails from guys that I've partied with who were virgins saying, "Thank you so much," and they tell me they are in a relationship, and "If I do this my woman likes it. . . ." I think it's great, you know, it gives you a sense of satisfaction.

JENNY: Do you have any emotional connections to any men that come in?

ASHLEY: No.

JENNY: Never?

MICHELLE: Not one.

JENNY: Wow.

ASHLEY: Never, not even like, "Oh, that guy's kind of turning me on." To be honest, it's all about money. All I see is dollar signs. We're having sex, and I'm counting how much I made today. I don't want him to leave his wife. I just want his money. I will please him while he's here, and he can go back and have a great life.

JENNY: What do you do when a really gross guy comes in and wants to have sex? Can you say "pass"?

MICHELLE: Here . . . yes, we can.

JENNY: And do you say it in front of him?

MICHELLE: Well, it's not what you say, it's how you say it. "You know, sweetie . . . I don't think we're gonna get along very well. . . . Maybe you should save your money and party with a girl who's gonna give you a good time." You know, something along those lines.

JENNY: What do you think about when you're having sex? I know I think about what groceries I have to get and things like that. Do you also do the same thing?

ASHLEY: As I said earlier, I think about the money. Can I get more from him? Can I extend the party? Can I do this? That's it.

JENNY: It's comforting to hear you talk about this as a business transaction.

ASHLEY: It's the only thing I'm here for.

MICHELLE: We're in a confined closed environment with a bunch of women, and you can't leave the property for a few weeks. . . . I just want to make my money, leave, and go home.

JENNY: Have you ever gotten so grossed out after one of the experiences? Cause I've slept with some guys that I wanted to vomit after.

MICHELLE: I wouldn't say grossed out. A lot of times it's mentally draining here, depending on if it's a fetish or a fantasy or some other type of party that you've already discussed ahead of time. It's really hard to go from beating the shit out of somebody in their fetish and then right back into the lineup.

JENNY: Do you think that all women should let their husbands get a professional at least once in their marriage?

ASHLEY: I, as a working girl, would say only if they are comfortable, because if you're insecure in any way, it's not gonna work. But if you reach that seven-year itch and want to spice it up, this could be a good anniversary present.

So there you have it! I can officially say I spent the night with two prostitutes. For all you ladies out there that might be on the kinky side and want to treat your man to a night of chicken for your anniversary, I can tell you they have the best legs and breasts in town. Thanks, Chicken Ranch!

20

Astrological Signs: Best Sex Partners According to the Stars

Who doesn't love to look up their astrology once in a while? Especially the part about love signs and compatability. (Although I've dated many guys who I'm supposedly compatible with and then realized I would rather date an elephant than go out with my "compatible" sign again.) I am amazed, however, that the description of my own sign really does match up with many of my attributes. Hopefully someday I can find the compatible sign in my life; in the meantime, have fun reading yours! (Sources: www.astrology.aryabhatt.com, www.stargazers.com, www.lifepsychic.com, www.starastrologer.com, www.extonbiz.com.)

CAPRICORN (DECEMBER 22—JANUARY 19)

In the bedroom: Capricorns are known to be very passionate and are willing to experiment to spice things up. They won't come up with the kinky ideas themselves, but they are willing to go along for the ride if their partner wants to do something.

Compatible with Virgo: Capricorns and Virgos have a high probability of a long-term relationship. They intuitively know their likes and dislikes. Capricorns love advice from Virgos, and Virgos are able to teach the Capricorn how to relax and take a load off. Capricorns possess a fierce ambition for success and tend to stay straight on their path to the spotlight. This drive for the spotlight is perfectly complemented by the Virgo's desire to please others, combined with the organized and meticulous nature of the Virgo. The Capricorn will have a partner that will assist in helping them achieve even more.

Compatible with Taurus: Capricorns and Taurus are clear-cut matches for each other. They want the same things in life, success and security. Both are very faithful and moral and are committed to attaining loyal life partners. The Taurus is much more straightforward and to the point, while the Capricorn is slow to reveal vulnerabilities and insecurities. Sometimes that can be misconstrued by the Taurus as "secretive," but the Capricorn's honest ways keep the Taurus feeling safe.

Least compatible with Aries and Libra.

AQUARIUS (JANUARY 20—FEBRUARY 18)

In the bedroom: There is never a dull moment in sex with an Aquarius. Experimental in every way possible, bizarre and quick to go on to his or her next exciting conquest, for the Aquarius each time must be a different position, if not a different person. Aquarians will follow the prospect of each new stimulating experience down whatever road that may lead to. They need to break new ground (or hymens), they need to do things "their" way and will not be tied down . . . unless a ball gag and whip are involved.

Compatible with Gemini: In order for the eccentric and creative Aquarius to enter a relationship, a strong foundation of friendship must first be established. Gemini adapt easily; they are intelligent but do not want to be the leader. The Gemini is open to the adventurous sexual nature of the Aquarius, and because the Gemini is up for the exciting journey, he or she will be able to sustain the other's interest. However, two impulsive spirits like these should be careful, because this much spontaneity doesn't always pan out smoothly.

Compatible with Libra: When an Aquarius and a Libra come together, the friendship that is so important for the

Aquarius to establish shines front and center not only to the two involved in the romantic relationship, but also to those in their social circle. Libras are incredibly indecisive, and love that the Aquarius is willing to step into the decision-making role. The Libra's indecisiveness could open the doorway to some kinky sexual experimentation, but it is the companionship foundation that binds these two, not the leather ropes.

Least compatible with Taurus and Scorpio.

PISCES (FEBRUARY 19—MARCH 20)

In the bedroom: Pisces are the first to put on a sexy nurse costume and give you a checkup. They are very giving sexual partners, and this could stem from their incessant need for reassurance. The need for constant pats on the back for jobs well done can take over a Pisces to the point where they stop experiencing the pleasure and completely disregard their own wants and desires. This often leads to a bad judgment in partners and leaves the Pisces aching for more sexual recognition. Pisces need a sensual, caring, attentive partner to please them and vocalize the great work they do on you.

Compatible with Cancer: Cancers are sensitive communicators that enjoy taking care of others. They are protective and would give anything to make sure their loved ones are safe and happy. Cancer and Pisces will help to stroke each other's egos. Both are water signs, lube may not be required.

Compatible with Scorpio: The Pisces is willing to give and please the Scorpio before himself/herself (in hopes of receiving praise for a job well done), while Scorpios feed on admiration and loyalty from those around them. Scorpios exude an intense display of emotion, and when that display of emotion is favorable or reassuring toward the Pisces, the Pisces gets his or her fix and will be content. Additionally, the Scorpio's needs are met by the Pisces's efforts to satisfy and openness to fantasy. Scorpios are strong individuals in every sense of the word; emotionally and physically they are in control and prefer to be with someone they consider a "weaker" partner so they can maintain that power.

Least compatible with Gemini and Sagittarius.

ARIES (MARCH 21—APRIL 19)

In the bedroom: Aries see themselves as leaders. They are aggressive, experimental, kinky, and can get bored quickly. They believe they know what needs to get done, and they will take control and dominate their partner to reach that climax they're chasing. They are in it for themselves and their best interests, and can be harsh on the road to getting what they want. Aries are not the best partners for the faint of heart. They have big egos and are full of adventure, a fire that will charm the pants off of you.

Compatible with Leo: Leos also see themselves as leaders, but they are also focused on a sense of fun and love for life and firmly uphold honor. They are strong enough to avoid complete domination by the Aries. It is important for them to have a family, and they want the best for those around them.

When Leos find love, the traditional romantic in them takes center stage (a place they like to be). If the two can work to find a compromise for control, they will avoid butting heads. The Leo's love for life and importance of loyalty feeds the Aries need for admiration and brings out the best in the Aries partner.

Compatible with Sagittarius: Aries and Sagittarius are both brutally honest, with a no-holds-barred approach to life. Sagittarians are wanderers on a quest for knowledge. While they can move around quickly, they move quickly with a purpose, which is focused on gaining answers to life's questions. They are the intellectuals of the astrological signs, and their thirst for knowledge could drive them into long-lasting conversations and relationships with an aggressive leader type that could provide the knowledge they so crave. Sexually, the Aries are more powerful, but if the Sagittarius can find useful information from these exciting sexual experiences, then all is good. But if the information is not found useful, the Sagittarius is quick to move on.

Least compatible with Cancer and Capricorn.

TAURUS (APRIL 20—MAY 20)

In the bedroom: Taureans are passionate, faithful lovers. They are affectionate and attentive to their partner, not selfish. While they can go for hours and hours, they are not into anal beads, vibrators, or playing dress-up. To get a Taurus in the mood, you have to rub him or her the right way with sensual massages and loving touches, and a good old-fashioned hot and heavy make-out session will seal the deal. Taureans prefer long-term monogamous relationships.

Compatible with Capricorn (also seen in the Capricorn section): Capricorns and Taureans are clear-cut matches for each other. They want the same things in life, success and security. Both are very faithful and moral and are committed to attaining loyal life partners. The Capricorn is slow to reveal vulnerabilities and insecurities. Sometimes that can be misconstrued by the more straightforward Taurus as "secretive," but the Capricorn's honest ways keep the Taurus feeling safe.

Compatible with Virgo: Virgo and Taurus is a conservative pairing. Virgos are more realistic when it comes to love, and once they have established trust within their partner, they will either be devoted for life as a romantic lover or, should the relationship end, continue their devotion in the form of friendship. Virgos need a little push to get heated in the bedroom, and the Taurean's sensual massages and intensely romantic physical contact give just enough push to get it going and then some.

Least compatible with Leo and Aquarius.

GEMINI (MAY 21—JUNE 20)

In the bedroom: Gemini says the more the merrier. They are open to swinging with multiple sexual partners. They are experimental, open to the new and the unknown territory that lies ahead. They are also intellectually driven, so their partner must be able to communicate and discuss anything and everything articulately, including their relationship and the adventures they take.

Compatible with Libra: Libra and Gemini stimulate each other. Jealousy is not an issue. Experimentation is welcomed, and communication lines are always open. Libras are very balanced and diplomatic, and Geminis are very easygoing in nature, so there will be lots of laughter, good conversation, and lightheartedness within this relationship. The main issue to look out for between these two is the openness to multiple partners; this can often lead to the ending of a relationship.

Compatible with Aquarius (also seen in the Aquarius section): In order for the eccentric and creative Aquarius to enter a relationship, a strong foundation of friendship must first be established. Gemini adapt easily; they are intelligent, but do not want to be the leader. The Gemini is open to the adventurous sexual nature of the Aquarius, and because the Gemini is up for the exciting journey, he or she will be able to sustain the Aquarian's interest. However, two impulsive spirits like these should be careful, because this much spontaneity doesn't always pan out smoothly.

Least compatible with Virgo and Pisces.

CANCER (JUNE 21—JULY 22)

In the bedroom: While Cancers are creative in the bedroom, they are first and foremost givers. They will not jump into any fantasy or begin pleasing their partner without a little guidance, but ask and you shall receive, and then some. The most important thing in the bedroom for a Cancer is that their partner is completely satisfied. Without fully satisfying their lover's needs, they will not climax themselves. Cancers are completely loyal, and honoring the relationship as an exclusive, monogamous one is vital for a future with a Cancer. Cancers can be very jealous and cling to their partner, so any hint at infidelity will not play out well.

Compatible with Scorpio: Scorpio is the master of his or her own destiny, strong and very sexual; they are a great partner to direct Cancer to satisfy their wants and needs in the bedroom. They are emotional, but because of the importance that Cancer puts on the relationship, the jealousy within Scorpio can lie dormant and avoid any eruptions. Additionally, once the Scorpio finds a loyal life partner, he or she will stay with that partner for a very long time. There is a lot of intensity between these two, whether emotional, physical, or spiritual.

Compatible with Pisces: Pisces are fueled by their emotions, and a sensitive, nurturing, caring, lover like a Cancer is a good match. They are protective and would give anything to make sure their loved ones are safe and happy. Jealousy and protective ways do not deter the Pisces, who so needs to be needed. Cancer and Pisces will help to stroke each other's egos. As both are water signs, lube may not be required.

Least compatible with Aries and Libra.

LEO (JULY 23—AUGUST 22)

In the bedroom: Generally Leo likes to be the center of attention, but they are happy to share the spotlight in the bedroom. While they are enthusiastic about sex, they are not too creative and tend to stick to the positions they are used to as well as the same initiation routine. If you want to slip something new into the mix, make sure you make it out like it was all the Leo's idea. Leos have big egos and like to play the "leader" role.

Compatible with Aries: Aries also see themselves as leaders, but the Leo is strong enough to avoid complete domination by the Aries. It is important for them to have a family, and they want the best for those around them. The Leo's love for life and importance of loyalty feeds the Aries need for admiration and brings out the best in the Aries partner. The Aries partner will also be adventurous enough to lead the Leo into more creative sexual encounters.

Compatible with Sagittarius: The leader within the Leo brings out the loyalty of the free spirit that is Sagittarius. Sagittarius is happy to let Leo be the leader; they want a stronger partner who can understand their free-spirited, independent ways. Sagittarians are willing to explore all avenues of all relationships, and they will also have some inventive sexual ideas to spice up the Leo's sexual behavior. It's been said that Leo is the only one that will be able to keep the Sagittarius from straying.

Least compatible with Taurus and Scorpio.

VIRGO (AUGUST 23—SEPTEMBER 22)

In the bedroom: Virgos prefer a more subtle approach and are not into the theatrics that some of the other signs enjoy. While the Virgo may be slow to get started, he won't be quick to finish. Virgos love passionate marathon lovemaking sessions. Virgos guard their most intimate feelings and emotions, and only a trusted companion or lifelong friend will be allowed to see that side of the Virgo. Once you have established trust with a Virgo, they will be devoted for life as a romantic lover or, should the relationship end, continue their devotion in the form of friendship.

Compatible with Taurus: Virgo and Taurus is a conservative pairing. The Taurus is a loyal friend and faithful partner, worthy of the trust given by its Virgo partner. Taurus and Virgo are a good match sexually because neither one is interested in creating a fantasy or going through any extravagant foreplay routines. The Taurean's sensual massages and intensely romantic physical contact gives just enough push to get the Virgo going and then some.

Compatible with Capricorns: Capricorns and Virgos have a high probability of a long-term relationship. They intuitively know their likes and dislikes. Capricorns love advice from Virgos, and Virgos are able to teach the Capricorn how to relax and take a load off. Capricorns possess a fierce ambition for success and tend to stay straight on their path to the spotlight. This drive for the spotlight is perfectly complemented by the Virgo's desire to please others and organized and meticulous nature, giving the Capricorn a partner that will assist in helping him or her achieve even more.

Least compatible with Gemini and Sagittarius.

LIBRA (SEPTEMBER 23—OCTOBER 22)

In the bedroom: When trying to pursue a Libra, you must pull out all the stops—candles, music, flowers, chocolates . . . you get the idea. If the mood is not right, the Libra isn't interested. It is important for everything to look perfect and harmonious. It is important for the Libra to be praised inside and outside the bedroom. They love to be praised, and perhaps in the case of the Libra, flattery will get you everything. The Libra will be open to spicing things up if you create the right atmosphere for it.

Compatible with Gemini: Libra and Gemini stimulate each other. Jealousy is not an issue. Experimentation is welcomed, and communication lines are always open. Gemini are easygoing in nature, so there will be lots of laughter, good conversation, and lightheartedness within this relationship. The main issue to look out for between these two is the openness to multiple partners; this can often lead to the ending of any relationship.

Compatible with Aquarius (also seen in the Aquarius section): When an Aquarius and a Libra come together, the friendship that is so important for the Aquarius to establish shines front and center not only to the two involved in the romantic relationship, but also to those in their social circle.

Libras are incredibly indecisive, and love that the Aquarius is willing to step into the decision-making role. The Libra's indecisiveness could open the doorway to some kinky sexual experimentation, but it is the companionship foundation that binds these two, not the leather ropes.

Least compatible with Cancer and Capricorn.

SCORPIO (OCTOBER 23—NOVEMBER 21)

In the bedroom: Scorpio is the master of his or her own destiny, strong and very sexual. The intensity that boils inside the Scorpio is unleashed in the bedroom. Sex with a Scorpio will probably be the best sex you've ever had! And I'm not saying that just because I am a Scorpio. The sexual partner of a Scorpio should expect to be dominated and open to new things. The biggest problem for the Scorpio is finding someone who will be a strong enough entity to be able to go up against the Scorpio and be fascinating enough to keep it interested.

Compatible with Cancer: Scorpios match up with Cancers because Scorpios have no problem directing the Cancers to their wants and needs in the bedroom. They are both emotional. The loyal nature of the Cancer keeps the Scorpio's jealous tendencies at bay. There is a lot of intensity between these two, whether emotional, physical, or spiritual.

Compatible with Pisces (also seen in the Pisces section): Because of the Pisces' willingness to give and please the Scorpio before himself/herself, in hopes of receiving praise for a job well done, the Scorpio feeds on admiration and loyalty from those around him. Scorpios exude an intense display of emotion, and when that display of emotion is favorable or reassuring toward the Pisces, the Pisces gets his or her fix and will be content. Additionally, the Scorpio's needs are met by the Pisces' efforts to satisfy and openness to fantasy. Scorpios are strong individuals in every sense of the word; emotionally and physically they are in control, and prefer to be with someone they consider a "weaker" partner so they can maintain that power.

Least compatible with Leo and Aquarius.

SAGITTARIUS (NOVEMBER 22—DECEMBER 21):

In the bedroom: Sagittarians are free spirits who truly like to make sure their partner is taken care of. Sex with Sagittarians is fun and exciting, never boring. While they are willing to experiment with toys, places, and imaginative situations, they are also willing to experiment with types of relationships as well. They are honest, and in order to have a successful romantic relationship, they will need an honest partner who will be open to adventurous sexual experiences.

Compatible with Aries: Aries and Sagittarius are both brutally honest, with a no-holds-barred approach to life. They are both spontaneous in nature and enjoy the same extravagant lifestyle choices. Sexually, the Aries are more powerful, but if the Sagittarius can find useful information from these exciting sexual experiences, then all is good. But if the information is not found useful, the Sagittarius is quick to move on.

Compatible with Leo (also seen in the Leo section): The leader within the Leo brings out the loyalty of the free spirit that is Sagittarius. Sagittarians are happy to let a Leo be the leader; they want a stronger partner who can understand their free-spirited, independent ways. Sagittarians are willing to explore all avenues of all relationships; they will also have some inventive sexual ideas to spice up the Leos' sexual behavior. It's been said that Leo is the only sign that will be able to keep the Sagittarius from straying.

Least compatible with Virgo and Pisces.

21

Cheating:
Thou Shalt Not Covet
Another Vagina

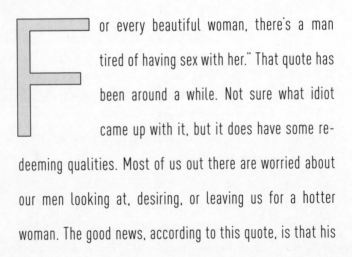

or every beautiful woman, there's a man tired of having sex with her." That quote has been around a while. Not sure what idiot came up with it, but it does have some redeeming qualities. Most of us out there are worried about our men looking at, desiring, or leaving us for a hotter woman. The good news, according to this quote, is that his long duck dong will eventually turn into a low mein noodle after time. As a result, we're forced to go deeper within relationships to find inner beauty and a soul connection that can get past flaws, fat, and hairy butts. Old people wouldn't have a chance in hell if all we cared about was having sex with hot people. Most young people would look at a seventy-year-old couple and think there's no way Grandpa wants to get it on with Grandma, but that's not true. He does! (And thanks to Viagra, he can.) Horny seventy-year-olds. Ew! Cheating stems from us thinking we are not getting something from our partner. According to my Twitter poll, in response to the question, "Why do we cheat?" the following excuses came back:

- He/she doesn't make me feel sexy.
- I'm bored.
- He/she never wants sex.
- I need excitement.
- I need an escape.
- I don't feel loved.
- I'm seeing if the grass is greener on the other side.
- My partner let himself or herself go physically.
- I cheated on my boyfriend/girlfriend to help me get out of the relationship I was in.

People tend to blame their partners for their cheating. Now that I'm older and a bit wiser, I find that hilarious. If you look closely at the excuses for why we cheat, they are always self-serving. Everything we do is for ourselves and no one else. I'm not making it up. Again, if you do The Work at www.thework .com, you will find that it's always about you and you alone.

A friend of mine, who has a ten-year-old son, disagrees with this point. "That can't be true all the time. I do things for my son, like take him to a good school to get an excellent education. That's for *him*," she told me recently. I answered, "Why do you take him to a good school to get an education?" She responded, "Well, because I want him to have ample opportunities in life." I responded, "Exactly my point. Look at that last sentence. '*I* want him to have ample opportunities.' Your child didn't ask you for it. You are doing it for *you*, but you *think* you are doing it for him."

I used that example first because it might be easier to swallow than husband-and-wife situations. It shows how we unconsciously blame everyone else for things we do, when it's always about us. Byron Katie is an expert in this area, so if it confuses you, please check out www.thework.com. So, let's get back to cheating, using that same theory. Let's look at the Twitter responses . . .

"He doesn't make me feel sexy, so I cheated on him. He should tell me I'm pretty and desirable more so then I won't have to go out and get it from other people. It's his fault." Let's dig in to that one, shall we? The girl is feeling like her man doesn't think she is sexy because he never tells her so. That could absolutely be true. He doesn't tell her, "You're hot, and I totally want to tear you up, baby." But what is really driving her to cheat is her own insecurity. That too is a hard one to swallow for many people, because who the hell wants to go in and uncover that pile of past insecurity shit? She used sex to fill that insecure hole in her heart and then blamed her husband for it. Is it the husband's fault that she has an insecurity issue? No. I'm sure he doesn't help the situation, but that insecurity belongs to her.

I brought this topic up at my sister's baby shower, and a Southern girl named Mary said, "My husband cheated on me four years ago." I responded, "You mean your ex-husband?" She said, "No, my husband." I replied, "Why in the world did you stay with him?" Which brings me to another issue with cheating. Why do girls stay with a cheater? I twittered this question to my girl tweeters and they responded with, "Because I still love him." I was amazed to find the majority still stuck it out with their man. Does this mean girls are weak, insecure, or secure enough with themselves to give love another chance? I asked Mary to talk about why she stuck it out. Here's what she said:

> My husband grew up in a really poor neighborhood in South Carolina. His parents were really religious, and there were a lot of demons within the walls of his home. There was a girl across the street who was the same age as him. He knew she was getting equally abused. Kevin [Mary's husband] longed for this little girl named Sue to be his girlfriend. When they reached the appropriate age to date, she moved

away and they never saw each other again. I knew this story
so well because Kevin brought it up all the time. It didn't
bother me. I thought it was sweet. I had been married four
years and had become pregnant with my second child when
my husband's past came knocking on the door. Not literally,
but with social networks pretty much anyone could be found.
Sue, his next-door neighbor, was passing through town and
asked if she could stay with us and catch up on life. I thought
it was sweet and felt bad that she was probably tortured in
childhood just as bad, and that maybe my husband and her
could talk about it and heal.

So Sue showed up, and we listened to her tortured stories
of how horrible it was growing up. She then segued into what
she does for a living now, which was working as a prostitute.
I thought that everyone deserves respect, so I let her stay.

She said they chatted the rest of the weekend and said their
good-byes. As the weeks went on, Mary's pregnant belly grew
bigger and bigger and her husband got meaner and meaner.
She couldn't understand what was going on. She figured maybe
because they were on their second child, her husband was feeling more pressure. He would yell at her for no reason, and then
finally he came clean. He admitted to having sex with the
hooker in their son's bed!

"Oh my God!" I exclaimed. "What did you do?"

She said that her husband was eaten alive by guilt and
couldn't hold it in anymore. Funnily enough, instead of kill-

ing him, she went after the girl. "I wanted to kick her ass, but I couldn't because I was pregnant. So instead I went into all of her accounts and changed her passwords and then would send numerous e-mails about how she destroyed my beautiful family. My daughter had just been diagnosed with Asperger's syndrome during this time, so leaving my husband wasn't really an option at this point. I just decided to torture Sue through e-mails. I guess it worked. I actually made her feel bad. She sent me an e-mail apologizing."

Mary forgave Sue in the end and then turned her attention to her husband. They fought like crazy, and every time they argued, she would throw the "You slept with a hooker" trump card and win the argument. If she asked him to run to the store and he said he didn't feel like going, she would come back with, "You slept with a hooker." Then he would go to the store. She would ask him to get up with the kids, he would complain that he was too tired. "You slept with a hooker." This went on for quite some time. Finally Kevin said, "Forgive me or let me go. I can't keep having you do this. I'm sorry, but can we please just get on with our lives?" They are still together and have worked in therapy to move past the infidelity, but she says that the pain of being cheated on will always linger in her heart.

Sandra Bullock and Jesse James, Tiger Woods and Elin Nordegren, are just the most high-profile of the latest cheating scandals. I don't know how either couple is going to be able to move on, but if I were Elin, I would use the "You slept with fifteen sluts!" scenario for a long, long time. I can't possibly guess why these men cheated, but based on the many male responses I received to my Twitter poll, it was about ego. Whether Jesse James's ego was hurt by his Hollywood power wife, or Tiger Woods had an egocentric need to fill his "I'm amazing-ness," we will never know. It belongs to them.

I haven't cheated on any guy since I was in my mid-twenties. I also have never been cheated on since then, either (as far as I know). I've come to the conclusion that if you feel the need to cheat, get out of the relationship or examine your thoughts and feelings as to what you think you are missing. Sex is fun for thirty minutes, but infidelity is tortuous for a lifetime.

22

Sex Facts:
Did You Know . . . ?

id you know . . .

. . . that sperm has vitamin B12 in it? It contains other stuff like fructose, various salts, and future children. The way some health freaks are, I wouldn't be surprised if they start bottling it up and selling it with other vitamins. Ew!

Did you know . . .

. . . that pigs' orgasms last for thirty minutes? That's insane! If reincarnation is real, I'm coming back oinking.

Did you know . . .

. . . that half of the men raised on farms have had a sexual encounter with an animal? Um . . . I take that last part back about wanting to be a pig in the next life.

Did you know . . .

. . . that the first known contraceptive was crocodile dung, used by the Egyptians in 2000 B.C.? It was replaced by elephant droppings, when they realized crocodile dung wouldn't work. Holy crap!

Did you know . . .

. . . that the word *avocado* is derived from the word *testicles*? Hahaha.

Did you know . . .

. . . that kissing can keep the dentist away, because saliva washes food from the teeth and lowers the acid that causes decay? Hmmm, so am I washing away food that was stuck in his gums all month?

Did you know . . .

. . . that the more sex you have, the more you will be offered? The sexually active body gives off greater quantities of chemicals called pheromones. These subtle sex perfumes drive the opposite sex crazy. I'd like to see Paris Hilton bottle that one and sell it. Actually, maybe not. One might need an antibiotic after applying.

Did you know . . .

. . . the sperm count of an average American male compared to thirty years ago is down 30 percent? Yikes, with that rate, in vitro could be a good stock to buy for the future.

Did you know . . .

. . . that sex burns 120 calories for a 130-pound woman every hour? Every hour! I'd rather grow a ton of cellulite than have sex for over an hour.

Did you know . . .

. . . that impotence is grounds for divorce in twenty-six U.S. states? Right on, girls!

Did you know . . .

. . . that dolphins are the only known animals other than humans that have sex for pleasure? (I wonder if they have hooker dolphins.)

. . . that male bats have the highest rate of homosexuality of any mammal? (So that's why Batman and Robin wear tights and are BFFs.)

Did you know . . .

. . . that only 17 percent of women can have orgasms during sexual intercourse? All others fake it. Then it's no wonder that sex feels like a chore most of the time!

Did you know . . .

. . . that 85 percent of men who die of heart attacks during sex are found to have been cheating on their wives? Karma is a real bitch.

Did you know . . .

. . . that the first couple to be shown in bed together on prime time television were Fred and Wilma Flintstone? Maybe that's because Fred was as hard as a rock. Hahaha.

23

Man Junk and Lady Bits

I asked my tweeters, "Why are we so attracted to boobs and penises when boobs are just clumps of fat and penises are clumps of tubing stuffed with blood?"

I was overwhelmed by responses from women who said they don't find penises attractive. I thought I was the only one! I'm so happy to hear that something that resembles an anteater's nose doesn't send all women into a frenzy. Women basically want to do things to the penis to turn on the man. We like the "doing," not necessarily the look or feel of it. My friend Chelsea Handler tells me that not everyone likes the "doing," and that I am particularly slutty for enjoying "doing" anything to it. Now don't get me wrong, penises do feel good, which is why we want to go skiing on them. But when a guy pulls out his man junk and waves it around or makes it throb all by itself, women are completely faking any excitement. We might go, "Oooooh baby, that's hot," but we are really thinking, Ew, it looks like a throbbing worm slug wearing a top hat.

Now, to be fair, let me tear into our lady bits. The vagina, which I like to call the canooter, has to be the second grossest looking thing, next to the penis. It's a bunch of skin all bunched up. I'm not saying men and women are not attracted to a canooter, I'm just saying it's not the prettiest girl in the class, if you know what I mean. Boobs and butts are curvy and sexy, but the canooter is just a hot mess that is almost impossible to maintain. It is ever-changing and ever-challenging. Sometimes, we are able to control it, and other times, it takes on a life of its own, just like a penis, but if possible, even more unattractive.

I'm also amazed that vaginas are all shaped so differently. Some girls have innies and some have outies. If you don't know what that means, please by all means Google an image. There's also a pretty enlightening Web site called RateMyMuff.com that shows you a picture of a girl, and you get to guess what kind of heat she's packing. This is not only informative, but a great way to burn a Saturday night.

Back in Chicago my girlfriend Mary and I went through

puberty together and shared any and every detail with each other. We were complete opposites, sort of like Laverne and Shirley; she was short and dark-haired and I was tall and blond. In any case, at one point she confided that she thought she had a tumor growth on her canooter. I told her to let me have a look. I was stumped by the extra flap of skin.

"What is that?" I asked.

"I don't know, that's why I'm asking you."

I pulled down my pants to take a look at mine. I had a button of stuff, but not the meat pillows she had. "Maybe you should go ask a doctor," I said.

"Oh my God, I have cancer."

"You don't have cancer. But it's definitely something. It just looks like some skin got caught in a machine, then got turned around and redirected, and then it got pulled . . . long."

"What the fuck are you talking about? It just grew like this overnight," she replied.

"Well, you need to go see a doctor," I said in an alarmed tone. Mary went off to the doctor's office and found out she had an "outie." When she told me the news, I once again pulled my pants down to check out mine. I guess I also had an outie, but nowhere near what she had. The next time we hung out, I asked her if she could ever wear jeans again, since her mud flaps might get bunched up. She replied, "Yes, actually, it does bother me. I have to move it or tuck it back inside when I wear jeans or work out. I also have problems riding a bicycle for too long. It's like I need an extra sidecar to put my groceries in." A few years ago she had surgery to get some roast beef sliced off, but it still has at least a quarter pound left. Labia reconstruction happens to be one of the most popular plastic surgeries going on right now. I spoke to one woman who had labia reconstruction, and right after they gave her the anesthesia, two cute male doctors walked in her room to talk with her about the surgery. "Horrifying," was the word she used to describe the experience. "Shouldn't there be an understanding that when you're getting one of the most humiliating surgeries available, the gender that you're trying to please doesn't make up the first two people you see in the OR?" she asked me. Who knew so many girls had canooter problems?

I started asking all of my friends in Los Angeles about their canooters. Half of them have outies and the other half innies. The majority of outies seem to have many more orgasms than girls with innies. Then I went and researched a bunch of guy forums and found many that talked about innies vs. outies and which they liked better. It was pretty much a tie down the middle. Some guys said that having something to nibble on was nice, and the other ones said they liked innie cuz it was smooth. Whatever the case, be proud of your lady bits. And if anyone has a problem with it, go get your situation reduced or tell him to go find a taco without the meat. The bottom line is, most men don't really care, and it's not like they're running out to get their penises fixed for us.

More funny/gross names for canooters:

Hot dog bun
Mammal hole
Fetus flaps
Afro clam
Prayer muffin
Mrs. Sphincter's next-door neighbor
Baby zipper
Bagpipe
Meat massager
Old catcher's mitt
Hairy harmonica
The toothless blowjob
And my favorite of all . . . front butt

24

Me So Horny

kay, ladies. I don't know about you, but it used to be that I only wanted my bell rung during ovulation. Which meant that the other twenty-five days of the month I was either needing a drink, or having to go through the motions to make my partners happy. This was so frustrating because I'm a Scorpio. We are sexual beings, but my bell wasn't ringing nearly as much as I wanted. I prayed to the universe for help, and then came a book by the name of *Breakthrough* by Suzanne Somers. She talked about hormone replacement and how well it worked in terms of

sex drive and mental stability during PMS and/or menopause. So I made an appointment with a doctor and was prescribed 50 milligrams of compound-grade progesterone. All I had to do, he said, was rub the cream on my forearm, day 14 after my period thru day 28. So off I went and started my cream. I shit you not, the stuff worked! I didn't fall into a murderous rage during PMS. I was calm. I felt a sense of peace within that I hadn't experienced since prepuberty. Then I started to feel my bell ringing again. Not only was I horny, but I had to take care of myself constantly or beg for it. I felt like a dog in heat but was so happy that I didn't have to have a glass of wine to get in the mood.

Now that I'm single again, I'm even more grateful that I got my hormones in balance. I did experience a problem with my dosage just last month, however, and experienced what it felt like to be a man for seven days. I started my new tube of cream and unbeknownst to me, I was putting too much on. The upshot was that I was so horny I couldn't even walk. I'm not exaggerating. I almost masturbated to *Celebrity Apprentice*. I kept saying to myself, Something isn't right. I found myself thinking about sex all day and night. My vibrator was so worn out, it actually started to make a screaming noise like it was getting eaten by a coyote. I called my best friend to ask her for advice. I was too embarrassed to call a doctor to tell him that I wanted to go hump a lamppost. My friend said that she goes through horny phases, but nothing that resembled my insanity. So days passed and I found myself writing this book and getting completely turned on. I even twittered about it. I then locked myself in my bathroom for three hours and had about fifty orgasms. That's so messed up, isn't it? I called my friend Chelsea, and all she had to say was, "You're a perverted loser." So another day passed, and the clock of horniness kept on ticking. I struggled to have thoughts that weren't about sex. If this is what men go through, I feel a little bit bad for them. (Only a little bit.) All joking aside, I was miserable because I couldn't function. I couldn't think. I couldn't talk to anyone. I even borrowed a Vicodin in hopes it would mellow me out. It didn't work. I was locked in a world of sexual fantasies, and I knew that if I masturbated any more, my uterus was going to fall out. But of course that didn't stop me. The crazy train of sex continued when I remembered about a cute guy-friend from out of town I've known for ten years. I decided to text him to see if he still had a girlfriend. Just my luck, he didn't. So I began sexting him. (Which I suck at, remember?) I was beyond forward in my messages and even insisted on flying to meet him for a quickie. How insane is that? After I made the arrangements, I decided it was time to call my doctor to see what the hell was wrong with me. I was scared to death because he was a very religious man. I decided to just be blunt as usual because this was an emergency situation.

"Hi doc, I don't know how to put this but . . . being a hooker never sounded so good to me."

"Um, how so?"

"Well, I'm so horny that I think I might die from it."

"Aren't you single now? Do you think that you could just be excited about dating?"

"I'm excited about dating, but this is abnormal horniness. My vagina feels like a venus flytrap that hasn't eaten in a year. I'm seriously dying. I can't even walk into the next room without having an orgasm."

(*Silence.*)

"Hello?"

"Yes, hmmmm."

(I can't even imagine what my doctor might have been thinking at this point.)

"Have you taken anything new that could have caused this?"

"No."

"Hmmmmm."

(WTF!!!)

"Well, it's obviously not normal. We will have to do some hormone testing."

"Oh, wait! I just started on a new container of progesterone. Could the bottle be a different mixture or something?"

"You could be getting a double dose without knowing it, which would cause this type of abnormal response."

(I love how doctors can put things into words that would normally be embarrassing. He said "abnormal response" instead of orgasming like a thirteen-year-old boy.)

"My dispenser seemed a little off this time, so maybe too much cream is coming out."

"Don't use any tonight, and let me know how you feel in the morning."

So I listened to the doctor's orders and skipped a night of cream and woke up with a peaceful vagina. I was able to start writing again and learned a valuable lesson in hormone replacement. Too much can turn you into a horn dog, but the right amount can bring back your sex life in a fun way. I'm still keeping the out-of-town booty call. I can't imagine what would have happened if I slept with him during this hormonal tornado. I think I might have broken his wiener. I'm sure I'll let you know how my booty call goes in an upcoming chapter.

25

The Perfect Booty Call

Okay, I couldn't wait to tell you.

I was less than a week away from the rendezvous with my friend in Arizona. I'll name him Mike for his own protection. Like he would really care. He would probably want me to put his first, middle, and last name in the book. I was really excited because I always thought he was hot, and whenever I hung out with him he was always just really cool and sweet. We both enjoyed each other's company but never had any opportunities to play Twister, as we were both in relationships.

Now that we were both unattached, I called him and said, "Listen, I want to be safe, so do me a favor and go get tested for STDs. I'll do the same." I was happy with his response, which was, "It's the only way to be." I set up an appointment with my gyno the next day to get tested. To my horrific surprise I woke up with my period. I wasn't due to get it for at least twelve more days. My hormone cream must have totally screwed up my cycle. I cried to my gyno to make it stop. He told me the only thing I could do was to use a diaphragm. I was horrified. I decided to just pray to the gods that my period would end before I met up with Mike.

But the day before I was supposed to fly out to meet him, my freaking period was still flowing like a faucet. I was having a heart attack because I had my flight and hotel booked, so I couldn't back out. I called up my hormone doctor and begged him for help. He had me come to his office, where he put these laser light machines on my belly in hopes his quantum infra ray light machine would zap my uterus closed.

I couldn't believe what I was putting myself through just to have sex. I know I am at my sexual peak and have waited ten years to have sex with Mike, so if I didn't give it everything I had, I would have been so pissed off at myself. After I left that doctor, I went to a Theta healer. Theta healers help you unblock belief systems that you hold on to. This early bleeding thing had to be some type of emotional blockage. So she muscle-tested me, and she said that I was scared of letting someone new into my heart. I replied, "No, I just want to let

Taken with my iPhone.

JENNY McCARTHY

him inside my vagina. My heart is under construction right now." She said, "Well, your muscle is testing positive for fear of getting hurt." Ugh, how annoying. She was probably right on a subconscious level. Our energy fields can be real assholes sometimes. She finally cleared that belief system, but I continued to go see one last doctor. He was an alternative medicine doctor. He listened to me ramble on about how my period must be stopped and giggled a few times at my desperation. He told me the only hope I had was to put on triple the amount of hormone cream, and that might just do the trick. He handed me the cream, and I sat in my car staring at this tube, thinking, Do I really want to mess with my hormones more than they already are? I threw the tube away and just prayed that my period would somehow magically disappear by the next day.

Once I got home, I began to make an iPod playlist for having sex. So I tried to think of all the songs that would have the right beat, and which weren't too cheesy. Hours had passed, and I had only purchased one song, "What Goes Around" by Justin Timberlake. I know it sounds childish that I was making a music playlist, but having the right environment is really important to me. Along with dark lighting and a penis that works. All very important things. So, now four hours had passed and I had only added two Rihanna songs to my playlist. My sister Jojo, who lives with me, was making fun of me because I was having such a hard time. She said, "Jenny, you can put on Clay Aiken and he would still f*ck your brains out."

I replied, "I would be horrified to have sex to a Clay Aiken song. I think my vagina would actually seal shut."

Jojo went on to say, "Just pick R&B songs. Black people know how to have sex." So with that, I downloaded three more Rihanna songs, Jay Z, and Alicia Keys. Jojo was right. After six hours of downloading my booty-call playlist onto my iPod, I went to sleep praying to the period gods that my vagina would be open for business.

I woke up the next morning, ran to the bathroom, and my period was gone. I couldn't believe it! Who knows which machine or spiritual healing worked on my uterus. I didn't care. Something had worked. I hopped on a flight to Arizona, and Mike was waiting for me at the gate. I was a little nervous because we had been friends for a really long time, and now I knew we were gonna do it. *Scary*, but fun.

Later that night I drank margaritas for the first time in my life. I had four of them and felt buzzed enough to go back to his place and get naked. I pulled out my iPod and hooked it up to his speaker and jumped in bed with him. He started kissing me, and I felt sixteen again. I would have been completely satisfied if the only thing we did that night was kiss. Okay, well, I think we all know that's not true. In any case, luck was on my side. Being that he is only thirty-six years old, all power tools were charged and working. Things were getting hot and heavy and just as he was about to reach orgasm, the next song started in, and I almost died. F*cking CLAY AIKEN started playing. JOJO PUT IT ON MY PLAYLIST!!! Oh my God, I wanted to kill her!!! I didn't know what the hell to do. Mike looked like he was almost there, so I didn't want to leap up and shut off the music. So I had the brilliant idea to moan louder than Clay was singing. I could tell from Mike's expression that he was confused as to why I was screaming so loudly. He kept saying, "You okay?"

"YES . . . OH GOD . . . YES!!" I shouted at the top of my lungs.

I had no idea what to say, so I just kept screaming the same thing over and over. Finally the damn song ended and I moaned a sigh of relief. Just then ANOTHER F*CKING CLAY AIKEN song came on!!!! I had images of murdering my sister. It was my first time back in the saddle, and I was having sex to Clay Aiken. Just when I thought things couldn't get worse, I heard Mike ask again, "Are you okay?"

I answered, "Yeah, great."

He says, "Well, you're kinda bleeding . . ."

"OH MY GOD!!! OH MY GOD!! I'M SO SORRY!!" With superhuman, cracked-out strength I flung the bedding over in one move and then ran out screaming. I was horrified!!! I was beyond embarrassed. First we had sex to Clay, and then I unleashed *Nightmare on Elm Street* sex. What a disaster.

The next day I was terrified to do anything. I didn't know what else could go wrong, so I kept my distance as much as possible. Again, I didn't seem to have my period, but I couldn't take the chance of having it magically reappear again. Toward the end of the evening Mike grabbed my face and kissed me. He slowly lowered me to the floor and took off my clothes. Ten years of waiting was the longest foreplay a girl could ever ask for. We had great sex, and I'm so grateful there was no Clay and no sign of anything else. It was just a beautiful night with an amazing friend. Finally . . . the perfect booty call.

26

Songs to Do the Nasty To

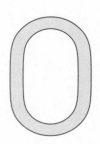kay, so here is a list of songs my tweeters say are their favorite sex tunes. Some of them I wouldn't be caught dead listening to, but everyone dances to the beat of their own drum. At the end of the list you will find my personal selection from my own iPod, labeled "Booty call."

Nine Inch Nails, "Closer"

Usher, "You Got It Bad"

Sade, "No Ordinary Love"

Sade, "By Your Side"

Scorpions, "No One Like You"

Kings of Leon, "Sex on Fire"

Pink Floyd, "Dark Side of the Moon"

Tool, "Push It"

INXS, "Not Enough Time"

Marilyn Manson, "Dope Show"

Deep Forest, "Deep Forest"

Avant, "Make Good Love"

Tricky, "Overcome"

Dave Matthews Band, "Crash Into Me"

Jordan Knight, "Give It to Ya"

Tenacious D, "F*ck Her Gently"

Jace Everett, "Bad Things" (Theme from *True Blood*)

Black Eyed Peas, "Sexy"

Need to Breathe, "Something Beautiful"

Janet Jackson, "Rope Burn"

Janet Jackson, "That's the Way Love Goes"

Keith Urban, "Raining on Sunday"

Led Zeppelin, "Whole Lotta Love"

Prince, "I Would Die for You"

Jeremiah, "Birthday Sex"

Toni Braxton, "You're Making Me High"

Lit, "My Own Worst Enemy"

Kings of Leon, "Closer"

Maroon Five, "Secret"

Alicia Keys, "You'll Never See Me Again"

Madonna, "Justify My Love"

Black Keys, "I'll Be Your Man"

Keith Sweat, "Nobody"

Led Zeppelin, "Dazed and Confused"

Lamb, "Gabriel"

Notorious B.I.G., "Hypnotized"

Deftones, "Digital Bath"

The Wallflowers, "Closer to You"

Usher, "I Wanna Make Love in This Club"

Black Crows, "She Talks to Angels"

Justin Timberlake, "Damn Girl"

Ne-Yo, "Addicted"

John Mayer, "Edge of Desire"

R. Kelly, "Bump N Grind"

TLC, "Red Light"

The Killers, "Mr. Brightside"

311, "Love Song"

Sarah McLachlan, "Possession"

Beyoncé, "Speechless"

Sade, "Cherish the Day"

Aerosmith, "Crazy"

Incubus, "Drive"

Sohodolls, "Stripper"

Goo Goo Dolls, "Iris"

Britney Spears, "Slave for You"

Massive Attack, "Angel"

My favorite responses: theme song from *The Colbert Report*, porn music.

JENNY'S IPOD "BOOTY CALL" PLAYLIST:

Rihanna, "Take a Bow"

Mary J. Blige and U2, "One"

Thievery Corporation, "Until the Morning"

Audioslave, "Like a Stone"

Clay Aiken!!!!!!! (f*cking Jojo!), "On My Way Here"

Clay Aiken!!!!! (f*cking Jojo again!), "Lover All Alone"

Justin Timberlake, "What Goes Around"

Fiona Apple, "Shadowboxer"

Fiona Apple, "Criminal"

Jay Z, "Empire State of Mind"

Hooverphonic, "2 Wicky"

Pras, "Dirty Cash"

Aaliyah, "Try Again"

Jay Z, "On to the Next One"

Alicia Keys, "Put It in a Love Song"

Jay Z, "Run This Town"

Timbaland (featuring Justin Timberlake), "Carry Out"

Garbage, "#1 Crush"

Alicia Keys, "No One"

Alicia Keys, "Fallin' "

Alicia Keys, "If I Aint Got You"

Alicia Keys, "Rude Boy"

Rihanna, "Disturbia"

Rihanna, "Hard"

Rihanna, "Umbrella"

Rihanna, "Rehab"

Rihanna, "Russian Roulette"

Rihanna, "Lemme Get That"

T.I., "Live Your Life"

Alicia Keys, "Un-Thinkable"

Lady Gaga, "Speechless"

Ne-Yo, "Because of You"

Chris Brown, "Forever"

David Guetta, "Getting Over You"

Danzig, "She Rides"

Portishead, "Glory Box"

Hess Is More, "Yes Boss"

Puscifer, "Rev 22-20"

Placebo, "My Sweet Prince"

Nouvelle, "Vague Psyche"

BitterSweet, "Drink You Sober"

Part Three

FAKING
IT . . . .

27

Boobies:
Just Clumps of Fat

woke up one morning and was getting dressed for fifth grade when I noticed the first bump of boobies beginning to grow. I was horrified. I didn't want boobs. They were stupid and silly looking and the boys made fun of them. To make matters worse, we didn't have much money so I was forced to wear my sister's hand-me-down bra. If you noticed, I didn't say bras. I said bra. I was allowed just one that my sister had used for two years and it was held together by a safety pin. I went to school hoping no boys would detect a bra line for fear of humiliation. Thank God for Carrie Dulewski. She took most of the attention away from the other girls during puberty due to her double-D breasts at the age of eleven.

The following year, my mom decided it was time for me to get my own bra. She came home from the JCPenney summer sale with my first very own over-the-shoulder boulder-holder. I ran upstairs, excited to try it on, and pulled it out of the bag. I took one look at it and burst into tears. It was a cross-your-heart grandma bra. It had crossover support as if it were holding up Mount Rushmore. I was barely an A cup. I had no choice but to wear it, because the other one had disintegrated into nothing.

Puberty was in full bloom when I met a boy named Jeff. He was a tough kid and not very nice, exactly my type. We went over to the house of my friend, whose parents bowled on Mondays, and snuck into a bedroom to make out. We were getting really hot and heavy when he started to undo my shirt. I couldn't wait for him to grab my boob. My hormones were raging and with each button that was being undone I imagined our wedding, our children, and how I would love this boy forever. He finally undid the last button of my school blouse and softly opened it. I arched my back in anticipation of his hand moving to cup my breasts.

"What . . . in . . . the . . . hell . . . is . . . that?" he said.

I opened my eyes, thinking he saw some sort of spider crawling on the wall. Then I noticed that his eyes were directly on my chest. He had a disturbed look on his face.

"What do you mean?" I said in my most terrified, this-could-scar-me-forever voice.

"It's a freaking grandma bra. It's so stupid looking. What a dork." In that instant, I turned into a shriveled, insecure, worthless little girl. He shouted to his friend to come in the room and check out what I was wearing. I pushed him off of me and ran home crying. He broke up with me the next afternoon. From that day on, looking sexy was my highest goal, held over anything.

By the time I left college, I had stuffed my twenty thousandth bra. I was so tired of those chicken cutlets girls wear that I was willing to do anything to get my boobs done. When you ask, you shall receive, because into my life walked an old friend with the most beautiful clumps of fat I had ever seen. I should say, clumps of saline I had ever seen. She had told me that she had found a doctor in Arizona who did boobs for fifteen hundred bucks.

"Does he do them in his garage? Why is it so cheap?"

"Dunno, but my tits look awesome."

She was right. They did look awesome. They were soft, round, and beautiful. I was determined to get back at boys like Jeff and prove to all future men that I was desirable. When I finally met with the doctor, I was grateful his office was not in his house or backyard trailer. He seemed extremely professional, so I decided to take my top off and show him my tiny goods. He stared at them for a moment and then poked around. "I think you should get a D cup."

I said, "Um, I don't want to go that big. I think C would be perfect." The doctor replied, "No, you have to trust me. Everyone always comes back to get them redone bigger. You should stick with a D." I pointedly replied, "No, I really only want a C cup." He finally gave up after a rather long back-and-forth. I don't understand why doctors and hairdressers don't just listen to what you want in the first place. Anyway, the day of surgery came, and I woke up with butterflies in my belly. I stared at my baby boobies, questioning if I should go through with it at all. I had thoughts of my Catholic mom at my funeral telling people I died for tits. But of course, vanity won over sanity. I was wheeled into surgery, injected with drugs, and slowly drifted off to the most bizarre dream of getting a boob job and hearing the doctors talk about it. I was thinking to myself, This is amazing that I happen to be dreaming about the exact same thing that is happening to my body. I was dreaming that they were tugging on my chest and pulling it. Then I opened my eyes and realized why I had only paid fifteen hundred dollars for this boob job. "I'm not under anesthesia!" I started screaming and tried to get up. "Jenny, just relax, we have one breast left."

I screamed back, "What in the hell do you mean I have one breast left?" I looked down and saw that one boob was big and one boob was small. "For the love of God, what have you done to me?!" I heard the nurse say, "Should we give her some Valium?"

"Valium? Valium? How about some fucking anesthesia?" I cried. They started on the other breast by putting a tool inside my breast pocket to make room for the implant. At this point I went into shock that I was allowing this to happen. I thought this kinda thing only happened in countries I couldn't pronounce. I looked down again, and the boob now matched the other one. I thought it was over until they grabbed my breast and violently moved it back and forth like they were pressing it into my rib cage. "Please, for the love of God, be done or give me drugs!!" Suddenly, the table I was lying on started making this electronic noise, and the table began to move into a standing position with me still on it. "Oh my God!! Please don't make me stand up and walk. I promise I'll stop yelling."

"Jenny, just relax. We have to make sure your breasts are even, so we need to stand you up," said the nurse.

I noticed that my arms were tied down but spread out like wings. "I'm gonna fall forward! You tied me up like Jesus on the cross so I can't even break the fall. Stop the table!" The doctor and nurse walked over to the other side of the room and stared at me like I was a ceramic bowl they'd just painted. I heard them agree that both the left and right boobs looked even. As a Catholic, being tied up like Jesus on the cross while naked and bleeding convinced me that this was punishment for my sins. I began to shout profanities that I'm sure Jesus would have said if he could, and then the miracle happened. I heard, "She's all done." Hallelujah! The electronic sound of the table started up, and I was lowered onto my back. They wheeled me out into a room and threw me on a La-Z-Boy to wait for my boyfriend to come get me.

I sat there in so much pain, completely pissed off I had gone through with it. I mean, why do guys like boobs so much anyway? When it comes down to it, they are just clumps of fat. Shame was the perfect word to describe how I felt sitting there on that La-Z-Boy. When my boyfriend walked in the room, he knelt down in front of me and I puked all over him. Thank God he was one of those boyfriends I could puke on, because little did he know he was going to be wiping my butt all week because I couldn't move my arms.

The only way I could describe the pain is, imagine a semi truck rolling over your chest and parking there for three days. That's exactly what it feels like. When we got back to the motel, I asked my boyfriend to hand me a pain pill. He looked at them and said, "Baby, they only gave you Tylenol." *What?!* I mean, come on, were these people sadistic? Because we were in Arizona we didn't know anyone, so I couldn't get any help. To make matters worse, I could only pay for two more nights in the motel and had to head back to Chicago on freaking *Tylenol*! Heidi Montag would have died if she experienced the pain I did. Anyway, we got to the airport and my boyfriend got out of the car to get me a wheelchair. I was so embarrassed because he had to put me in the damn thing and leave me sitting there while he returned the rental car! I hadn't bathed, my hair was in knots, and I was grimacing in pain. To make matters worse, I couldn't move my arms, and my boyfriend left me in a high-traffic area. Seeing the pity in people's eyes was worse than being awake during surgery. I started to get angry and yelled,

"Take a picture, it will last longer," which I'm sure made me sound like a third-grader in a wheelchair.

At least an hour had gone by, and I began to assume the worst: my boyfriend had left me at the airport to rot in hell. Why wouldn't he have? I'm sure he didn't appreciate my period coming early and my inability to move my arms. Then in the distance my man showed up and saved me. He got me to the gate, where they had told him he needed to board without me and that I had to board last. He explained that I needed extra help because of my condition, but they didn't seem to care. They said that airport people would help me. So my boyfriend kissed me good-bye and boarded the plane. Now what kind of freaking airline has that as a rule? Usually those who require "extra assistance" get to board first. (Looking back, I realize that in my life I have always experienced the opposite of normal; at least I have good stories to tell when I'm drunk. And other people do, too.)

Everyone boarded the plane, and it was finally my turn. I was a tiny bit excited, knowing I would be in my own bed soon. They took me outside, and I saw that there wasn't a jet bridge. It was one of those stair things they push next to the plane in lieu of the jet bridge. How was I going to climb all those stairs? I could hardly even stand. Two guys in airport jumpers approached me and said, "Do you think you can make it?" I said "Hell no, I had surgery."

"Where?" they replied.

"Ummmmm . . . in my chest." I think they thought I had

heart surgery or something because they gently grabbed each armpit and held me in the air, pulling me up the stairs. I was in so much pain with every step that I was literally howling like a coyote. I made it into the plane, where everyone was staring at the crying handicapped girl who just boarded. They sat me next to my boyfriend, and we prayed the worst was over.

We took off and the turbulence was out of control. Everything was bouncing around, and I asked the flight attendant for extra pillows to encase my body. She was very sweet and surrounded me with pillows and then kindly asked what surgery I had done. I told her I got my boobs done, because I felt like a woman could relate to the insecurities of a girl. I swear to God she turned into an evil bitch before my very eyes. If she could have snatched the pillows back she would have. Hours went by, and my mouth was parched. I had my boyfriend ring the bell to call them to see if I could get some water. "No, not right now, there is too much turbulence." But if I were a handicapped girl you could be sure I would have gotten a case of water delivered to my seat.

We finally made it home, and I took off my bandages after a week and almost died yet again. My tits were huge. Yes, they were swollen, but I knew after the swelling went down I was going to be a D cup. Well, the swelling went down, and I was right. The bastard gave me a large D cup. Then because of the stretching, a month later I woke up with the worst stretch marks known to mankind. I mean bad. I kept bitching to my friends and they said, Show us in the bathroom. So I showed them and they said, "Oh my God, that's awful." Three years later I went back, to the same guy, to get my boobs the size I wanted, a C cup. But I'm still painfully insecure about my boobs. I don't have sex with the lights on and hope one day either that I can become okay with them or that a cream will come out that regenerates new skin.

Do I regret that I did it? Well, I try not to regret anything I do. You can't change the past, so why bitch about it? I just wish I'd waited until I got older to see if boobs really mattered. They don't in my eyes, but to some guys they do. I can see their point. I don't like small penises.

Before I end this chapter, I have to tell you that I bumped into Jeff, the boy who made fun of my bra, at a bar while I was on *Singled Out*. He came up to me and said, "Wow, you really grew up hot. I can't believe it. Do you want to dance?"

I smiled and said, "Sorry, I don't dance with dorks."

28

The Facade:
Love the Fake Me

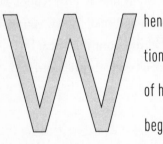Whenever I look back at past relationships, I cringe when I think of how perfect I tried to be in the beginning. Laughing at dumb jokes, acting like a lady, farting in the other room, pretending I like to watch football when I would rather be getting a root canal. This is incredibly common in all relationships. We work so hard to win the approval of our new partner, their friends and family, that we lose touch with

who the hell we are. We don't live our lives . . . we are acting them instead.

What winds up happening as a result is that by the time our partner tells us they love us, we get angry inside because they actually fell in love with our pretend self. We morph into who we really are, and our partners think we have changed. But we're truthfully showing them for the first time who we really are.

I even had this happen in my relationship with you. Yes, you reading this. I had a facade that I was this ball-busting, tough, belching, loud cheerleader on this show called *Singled Out*. This is not how I am in my everyday life. When I auditioned for the show, I tried to figure out what hadn't been seen in a hot chick on TV. No pinup had dared to make fun of herself the way I did, so I played the act and became really famous for something I was not. Living up to that facade was hard on me. Everywhere I went people wanted me to punch them in the arm or stick my tongue out. Every red carpet I went to, the photographers would scream at me to pick my nose in the picture. I thought this was how I would win your approval, your love. I thought girls would like me more because I wasn't trying to be hot. It worked because it was a breath of fresh air to see a girl belch and not care what she looked like. But I became so tired of the act that it began to make me crazy. Every magazine I would open up, I was making a wacky face. I kept talking about being this free-spirited, wacky, fun chick, when all I did was sit at home every weekend and play chess with my fifty-year-old boyfriend.

Then one day I woke up and said, Enough! I went out to a red carpet event, and the photographers shouted, "Do something crazy, funny." I replied, "No, I'm all done with that." They slowly put their cameras down and refused to take my picture. I was in shock! Even my date was in awe of the protest the photographers were making. I stood my ground and posed like a normal human being. Maybe one flash went off before I moved on. This went on for two years. Every red carpet I went on, I fought with the photographers to let me just pose pretty. I didn't show up in magazines for two years, and it got to the point where people would say to me, "Do you work anymore?"

It's just like in a real relationship when you start to reveal who you really are, and your boyfriend might not like the true you. He might get angry that you had changed. That is what happened in my career, and it was devastating. I decided that when I made any sort of a "comeback" I was just gonna be real—even if I seemed boring, even if people didn't like it.

Pamela Anderson is another prime example of this phenomenon. Her pretend self is the sexiest woman in the world. We expect to see sex dripping down her fingernails all the time. If she had cut her hair and made her boobs smaller ten years ago, would we still like her? Who knows? I think we can all tell she is struggling in her forties to hold onto the facade of being the sex kitten we all want her to be. This is in no way an insult to Pam. I like her. I have seen the side that you don't see, and she is the "no makeup sweatpants Mom" who is completely normal, but she wouldn't dare drop the facade for fear of your disapproval. Hopefully, one day she will feel safe enough to.

Let's examine the pretend self a little more . . . What the hell are we so scared of? What's the worst that could have happened if we had answered honestly instead of all the lies we tell our new boyfriends at the beginning of a relationship? "No, I don't really like basketball." Maybe his response would have been, "Okay." Wow, can you imagine? He might have been fine with the truth. Let's move to the next one, "I don't really like your crazy aunt." He might have just said, "Yeah, me neither." And we could have laughed about it instead of listening to the crazy bitch talk about her chest infection. Let's do the next one: "I really don't want to miss my girls' night out." He might have been bummed, but I also suspect that he would have found the honesty more of a turn-on than if I had stayed home with him.

I'm in the painful process right now of revisiting my behavior at the beginning of each relationship I ever had. And like I said in the beginning of this chapter, sometimes it's embarrassing to live through it again. But the more I look back, the more I become aware of what I did and the joy I sacrificed as a result. Hopefully now I will be able to recognize when my pretend self pops up in a relationship and stop myself from trying to trick my future man into thinking I'm perfect. I hope, just like in my career, I can feel okay with being liked by some and hated by others. Authenticity makes the world a better place.

29

Aphrodisiacs: So We Don't Have to Fake It!

aph·ro·di·si·ac

Pronunciation: \ ,a-frə-'dē-zē-ak, -'di-zē-\

Function: *noun*

1: an agent (as a food or drug) that arouses or is held to arouse sexual desire.

1. Bat Meat

In Indonesia and Malaysia bat meat is one of the most popular ways to get things rockin' in the bedroom. It's easy to find (usually at your local supermarket or from street vendors), and costs virtually nothing. It's the street hot dog of the East. But we're not talking about making the bat into some nice tangy spread to put on crackers;

you eat the whole thing—head, wings, and all. Not unlike a lobster dinner. Yum.

2. Rhinoceros Urine

If you're still waiting to experience that mind-blowing night of sex and you don't really care what you put in your mouth, then India or Nepal is the place for you. It's here that you can purchase a cup of rhinoceros pee at the Kathmandu Zoo. You'll find it right next to the T-shirts and souvenir DVDs. The animal keepers there collect the fresh pee every single day and make sure it's bottled quickly to guarantee purity. Just drink a glass shortly before having sex, and turn a regular old night in the sack into a mind-blowing jungle boogie. But don't forget to bring mints.

3. Big-Bottomed Ants

Colombia, South America. These critters are apparently such an awesome aphrodisiac that people give them as wedding gifts to help the just-married couples get off to a good start. Word is they taste great roasted.

4. Snake Blood

Poisonous varieties are preferred. Bangkok bartenders are more than happy to stir some snake blood into plain water or rice wine to make it more palatable. But if you're a real man (or woman), then slurping the blood straight from a newly made puncture in the snake's tail is the way to go. Apparently, the effect hits you in under ten minutes, so wait until after church or that important presentation to drop some.

5. Reindeer Antlers

Reindeer antlers, huh? I guess now we know why Santa Claus has such a big bag. In Scandinavia, arguably the best place besides the North Pole to find a reindeer, locals grind the antlers into a fine powder that is dissolved into hot water a couple of hours before pork time. And the rep for this boner juice is so high that people as far away as China pay Bill Gates–size amounts just to import it.

6. Spanish Fly

Spanish fly is, yes, a Spanish fly. One of the oldest known aphrodisiacs, this roach has been used for enhancement of the male organ for centuries. Once you consume one of these babies (crushed up, of course), it's excreted into the urine and causes the genitals (or in medical terms, the shlong) to swell to enormous size and stay that way for hours. Who needs Viagra?! When taken by women, it supposedly causes a mild itching sensation down there that can be confused with sexual arousal. It's either that or crabs.

7. Rhino Horn

Rhino horn is commonly believed to have originated as an aphrodisiac in Chinese folk medicine, but it's a popular getter-upper in India as well. Usually it's taken with a bit of honey. I would hope so. Otherwise how would you get that thing in there?

8. Oysters

Raw oysters as horny potion date back as far as ancient Rome. Some believe that this started because of the oyster's resemblance to the female naughty bit. If my female naughty parts looked like a raw oyster, I think I'd die. Taco, yes. Oyster, not so much. Even though there is no proof that oysters work as an aphrodisiac, they can be fun to slurp on a first date.

9. Sea Cucumber

You wish this were an actual cucumber that grows at the bottom of the sea, but noooooo! It's a huge, sausage-shaped sea creature that stiffens and squirts fluid when disturbed. Sound familiar? In China, this male performance enhancer is cooked into what basically amounts to something like pork fat, which is then spread on crackers. It can't be consumed whole. That wouldn't look very macho.

10. Balut

In the Philippines, you can buy this aphrodisiac right off the street. The name may sound like some kind of Polish doughnut treat, but it's wayyy not. It's a duck egg that contains a fetus about twenty days into gestation. The egg is tapped, flipped upside down, you drink the liquid, then peel the egg to reveal part of a duck fetus and the occasional feather. Okay, you can go throw up now.

11. Wolf Meat

In Mongolia wolves are a popular aphrodisiac, especially in the winter. When consumed, the diner has been known to experience a "warming effect" throughout the body. It's easy to see how this could be associated with jump-starting the sexual appetite. Someone should introduce Hot Pockets over there and save the species from extinction.

12. Fugu, aka Blowfish

One of the most poisonous fish in the sea, the fugu or blowfish is considered one of the most potent aphrodisiacs in Japan. Some people believe that it's the tingling sensation you get from eating the nontoxic part that gives you the sexual rush; others claim that it's the fish's testicles that have been soaked in sake that really do the trick. In any case, make sure you get a licensed sushi master to prepare it for you because one bite of the poison part, and you're dead meat.

13. Tiger Penis

In China, Taiwan, and South Korea, the most sought-after "tool hardener" is, sad to say, tiger penis. In theory it's supposed to increase male stamina when consumed, but all it really does is decrease the already dwindling tiger population.

14. Green M&Ms

Green M&Ms have been considered an aphrodisiac since the early 1970s. Not surprisingly, green M&Ms are the only color that still remains from their debut in 1941. Damn, and I've been eating the red ones the whole time.

15. Placenta

Many people, and not just dirty hippies, believe that eating the afterbirth will catapult their sex drive into orbit. Sheep placenta is even sold over the counter in stores across Asia for this specific reason. But hey, even if it doesn't put lead in your pencil, it's still a nutritious start to a great day!

16. Love Stone, aka Toad Venom

This aphrodisiac has probably killed more people than it's gotten laid. The Love Stone, which is basically toad venom, comes from the West Indies but is really only still used in China. Take the wrong amount of this stuff, and that fun time you're having is going to be your last.

17. Urine

Pretty much any kind of urine will do. Baboon urine is mixed with beer in Zimbabwe. Cow urine straight up is pretty popular in India. People have even been known to drink cat urine just so they can have a wild time in the sack. But probably most popular is the human kind. It's sometimes taken from people who are high on hallucinogens to give it that extra kick. It's even sold in some grocery stores and usually comes with a free toothbrush. Okay, that last part isn't true. But it should be.

18. Ambergris

Sounds like some sort of precious gem, right? Well, it isn't. Ambergris has been utilized for centuries as an ingredient in perfume, but its most popular use is as one of the world's most sought-after aphrodisiacs. What is it? you ask. Why, it's sperm whale vomit, of course. If that doesn't get you hot, then I don't know what will.

19. Soup Number 5

If you find yourself in the Philippines and you're in need of a sexual pick-me-up, just order Soup Number 5 at the nearest restaurant. And if they don't know what you mean, just tell them you want the soup made of bull penis and testicles. The sexual enhancement properties of this tasty dish are legendary.

30

Lights Off in the Bedroom!

ost of us have body issues that drive us crazy. The only person I can say probably doesn't is Giselle the super-model. She might have the most amazing body on the planet, but God probably gave her really bad period cramps, cuz no one is getting off that easy. For the rest of the female population, body issues plague our thoughts whenever we try on clothes in front of a mirror, wear swimsuits on the beach, and of course during sex.

Keeping the lights on during sex exposes every flaw, leaving some of us vulnerable and depressed. It's when I become most paranoid about myself because I don't want any man to be less attracted to me—especially considering the fact that I'm getting older. A guy can go score a twenty-year-old whose canooter was not blown out by a baby. I also ballooned up to 211 pounds on my last day of pregnancy, so I can relate to insecure body issues.

I really envy women who are on the bigger side and have confidence that they are 100 percent hot—lights on or lights off. To me they are sexier than Giselle. Guys are attracted to confidence, and if we can just get ourselves to be like that, we might be okay with a little junk in our trunk. And I guarantee our men would be, too.

Personally, I don't think guys care that much. They are so horny most of the time that I don't think they notice. Sure, they get a boner watching a Victoria's Secret commercial, but odds are they are never gonna get one of those models, so why do you care?

I'm not saying I look disgusting. I know I have a good body, but my skin is not the same, with all the stretch marks. It's awful! And gravity doesn't help things either. My boobs are so droopy that if I don't wear a bra, I'm afraid I'm going to accidentally flush them down the toilet when I go pee.

What men, who are also aging in the bedroom, need to realize is that having the lights off during sex is beneficial to *them* also. Men have a tendency to get a little big in the belly, and what usually follows are man-titties—which are far worse than any amount of cellulite a girl could ever have. If I wanted to see boobies shake in my face during sex, I would be a lesbian. In the meantime, boys, lights off during sex if that sounds like you.

The other benefit to a dark room is that I can imagine myself hot and naughty. I can bend in positions that can make me seem like the slut he hopes I am in bed. I have noticed though, as I get older, that I have zero interest in trying to fake being turned on. I want to be lusted over, and I want to lust over him. When you don't feel lustful in bed while having sex with your man, it can actually feel like you're getting raped. I know that sounds harsh, but I mean it in terms of "taking one for the team" when you're not in the mood. It truly is amazing how painful sex can be when it feels like a chore. I still think it's cruel that we weren't born with the same sex drive as men, but statistics say men usually die before women, so I guess we get one bonus in the death department.

Now, don't get me wrong, I'm sure there are some brave souls out there who enjoy watching the sexual act with the lights on. I have one girlfriend who says she doesn't care either way. But she also doesn't have a C-section scar with fatty tissue hanging over it. I have no idea how porn stars do it. They are under the hottest lights and usually have to contort themselves into positions that are unflattering for most humans. I'll go with my mom's point of view on this one, which is, "They are high, and that's why they don't care." That's actually not a bad idea. Have a little drink if you think your man is gonna want to do it outside at high noon.

Overall, I think a great compromise in the lighting battle is to dim the lights or use candles. Not only is it romantic, but it really does give nice shading to older skin. Sure, it's a kind of faking, but that doesn't matter—I need to feel good for me, otherwise I'm gonna fake more than the lighting.

31

When Botox Goes Bad

I was standing backstage waiting for my name to get announced for the first episode of a new talk show, *The Megan Mullally Show*. (It's no longer on air, and I can't help but wonder if that had to do with me.) As I stood there waiting, I tried to do as many mouth exercises as I could. I looked into a mirror backstage and saw drool coming down the side of my mouth. "Oh Gawd! What da hell em I gonna do?" Jojo, who does my makeup, looked at me and said, "You look like a stroke victim!"

The lights brightened, and I heard, "Please welcome Jenny McCarthy!" I shouted to Jojo, "Quick do sumpting!"

She replied, "Maybe you should of thought of that before you froze your entire chin with Botox." The stagehand pushed me out into a glaring bright light, and as I walked onto the stage I saw these huge grins on the faces of the audience; they couldn't wait to see what wacky crazy thing I was gonna talk about. My heart raced as I got closer to Megan, who gave me that familiar TV host look: "Bitch, if you fuck this up, I'll kill you." Thoughts of double-page spreads in every gossip magazine—"Jenny Mc-Carthy overdoses on Botox; loses ability to speak"—flashed through my head. I took a seat opposite the host and listened to the clapping die down. "Jenny, it's so great to have you here," the host said.

Oh my God, I'm supposed to speak now? What am I gonna do? Should I faint? Yeah, I should faint! But then everyone will think I'm on drugs. Maybe I should run off and pretend I have the stomach flu. No, cuz people will still think I'm on drugs. Shit. God, please help me. I slowly blinked my eyes and felt a rush come over me that felt like an angel had just picked me up and dropped me off in heaven. When I opened my eyes, I was shocked to find myself standing inside a cloud in the sky, looking directly at God. He resembled Jesus, but just a little bit chubbier and hairier.

"God, please help me. I'm supposed to speak right now on TV, but I can't because my chin is frozen. Wait, my chin is not frozen anymore!"

God replied, "That's because you're in heaven right now, idiot."

"Am I dead?"

"No, I give one pass in a lifetime to people who are about to ruin their lives. And you are about to ruin your life."

"Jesus Christ."

"No, it's God," he replied.

"What are you gonna do?"

"Haven't figured it out yet," he said.

"Well, I think people are kinda waiting on me."

"Jenny, what in the hell made you go to a doctor and get your entire chin Botoxed? I mean, let's get real for a second. Who does that? I can see your forehead, but your chin?"

"God, I started to get these two dents in my chin, and when I mentioned them to the doctor, he told me I could Botox it to make it go away."

"I gave you those dents. Why would you *not* want something I gave you?"

"Well, let me get real with you now, God. Why in the heck would you give women wrinkles in the first place? We already have to go through childbirth, we stay up with the babies, we are exhausted, our boobs sag, we get wrinkles, and many husbands cheat on us because we get frumpy. Why couldn't you just give us a break in the wrinkle department?"

"Listen, you are the stronger of the two human forms. I knew you women could handle almost anything and personally . . . I like saggy boobs."

"Well, that's because you're like one hundred trillion years old."

"Go to hell."

All of a sudden the clouds parted, and I fell through them. I began screaming and continued to scream until I hit a hard surface. The wind was knocked out of me, and I struggled to get my bearings. It was dark and gloomy. All of a sudden a shadowy figure approached. He looked familiar. Oh my God, it was Satan!

"Greetings, my insecure one!"

"Satan, what za hell em I doin here? Oh no, I canth talk again."

"Well, you are obviously caught up in your looks, and I couldn't be more proud. I think you look fantastic, by the way. Those wrinkles in your chin really did disappear."

"Weally?" I ran over to a mirror in Satan's dojo and began screaming in horror. My chin looked liked Jay Leno's! "You canth weave me like tis."

"Leave you like what? . . . beautiful? You are destined to be my second best student!"

"Who's your first?"

Suddenly a body came down from the ceiling and landed in a loud *frump*. Once the smoke cleared, I saw that it was Joan Rivers.

Satan said, "She is."

Noooooooooooooooooooooooooo!

I closed my eyes, and when I opened them again I was sitting across from the host, who repeated her sentence, "Jenny, it's so great to have you here." I realized at that moment that it was inevitable: I must surrender to the gods of aging and be comfortable with some wrinkles in my life. In the meantime, I had to get through this interview. I drew on the same strength that people use if their baby is trapped under a car and they lift it with one hand. I moved my mouth with all of my might and replied, "It's great to be here."

I did it. I said a sentence! Now I only had six minutes of talking to do. Throughout the rest of the interview I spit on the host at least thirteen times and sounded like I had a lisp. I was happy with that. Once I got backstage Jojo looked at me and said, "You're an embarrassment to our family." I knew Jojo would get over it. I was a few years older than her. No doubt Satan's potion would beckon to her at some point, too.

32

Women: The Masters of Manipulation

I thought only evil girls manipulated men to get what they want. Oh no, Charlie Brown, we *all* do it! I was first made aware of this when I sat down with a therapist shortly after moving to L.A.: "You know you manipulate guys by testing them to get what you want." I was shocked. How dare she say such an awful thing?! She said, "Think about everything you told me and try to find it." So I flashed back to what I had told her, and it hit me like a ton of bricks. Holy crap, Batman! I was a master of manipulation!

I moved to Los Angles in 1994. By 1997, I had moved in with this guy named Paul. I had a really hard time adjusting to his house because of course it was *his* home. I didn't feel like I belonged and never felt truly at home there. I roamed the halls afraid to leave my shoes in the corner. I also noticed I would start hoarding and holding on to boxes of junk in the guest room so I felt like I actually had something of mine in the house. I know this sounds so stupid, but it was real to me, and it will give you a good idea about how we unconsciously manipulate, so just hang in there with me.

So . . . within the first week of moving in, I said to Paul, "We need a new mattress." He answered with a perfect guy response: "Yeah, eventually." I immediately went into an internal mind spin and thought, I don't have a say in the house. I'm just a guest. I feel worthless, and I don't belong here. I really started to believe these thoughts because, as the spiritual teachers teach us, once we believe our thoughts, they do become our reality. And for three years I roamed those halls believing, I don't belong here, I don't feel welcome. So unconsciously I began to test him. Again, I wasn't aware of this until the therapist woke me up to it. My sob story to her was, "Paul doesn't make me feel like I'm at home; Paul doesn't let me do anything in the house. Wah wah wah wah wah wah." And then I looked at how I tested him to prove to me that I belonged in his home. I walked him to the living room one day and said, "It really looks like an old lady died in here. No one wants to sit in this room ever. Can I change it? I don't want to buy anything. Let me just move all the furniture around." Paul answered, "I think it's fine just the way it is, babe." *Ahhhhh.* My insecurities were going nuts.

Then I tried something easy, or so I thought. I took down some of his pictures to hang some that I liked. He got upset with me because he thought they belonged in a different place in the house. He said his dead mom was always on that wall, and to move her would be wrong. I pleaded, "But she won't know she was moved because she's dead, baby!" He stormed off with a strong, "No!" This threw me into another "I don't belong here, this isn't my home" tailspin. At night, I was like a hamster roaming from room to room, imagining how I would change things.

Because of my "issues," I started holding resentment toward Paul. I would be sitting across the room looking at him while he was watching TV, and have so much anger because I just wanted to feel at home. Poor guy had no idea! Looking back now, I can't believe how much energy I wasted trying to test Paul into proving I belonged in his home. I was driven to get my mission accomplished. I thought to myself that even dogs pee on their surroundings to mark their territory. It's human nature. I pictured myself going outside and peeing on a bush. Again, I was completely oblivious to the fact that I was testing him. I really thought that I simply wanted to redecorate, and that Paul was being stubborn.

So . . . I started to up the pressure and got my friend to pose as a decorator to come in and do a quote. I showed Paul what the designer was going to do to the living room, and he said, "That's too much money." I replied in perfect manipulative form: "No, I'm gonna pay for it." Wow, I thought, there is no excuse now. This will prove now that I belong here. This will make me feel like I'm home if he allows me to do this. I'm paying for it, not him. So there's no excuse . . . or so I thought. He replied, "We're having Christmas at my house this year, and I don't feel like dealing with construction." Dammit!!!!!!

I failed again. Now, I don't want you guys to think I was doing this to him every day for three years. It was sporadic, flaring up whenever I felt unworthy of being in his home. That's when Jenny "Martha Stewart" McCarthy would rear her ugly head and find anything to change in the house. And to answer the question I hope you guys are asking by now—Why was Paul being so stubborn about his place? Why wouldn't he just let you redecorate a room?—believe it or not, the reason doesn't matter, because I was still trying to manipulate him into proving that I belonged there. If I kept blaming him, I would never get to the problem of it being *my* problem.

Then after three years of living together he said to me, "You know, it does kinda look like an old lady died in the living room. Go ahead and change it." I couldn't believe it. Oh wow, that should make me feel at home now! I walked out of the room with a big smile on my face. Within minutes, however, I felt the smile fade. After three years of trying to test him into letting me change the house, I still had that sense of not feeling at home. WTF? This was supposed to be the answer to all of my worries. Weeks went by, and I did nothing with the living room. I would walk past it and think, I don't want to redecorate. I hate decorating. Paul kept asking, "Did you start to pick things out?" I would answer with, "No, I've been really busy." Which was total bull. I was numb and confused as to why I didn't want to redecorate, and why I still felt out of my element. Which brings me back to the shrink:

"Jenny, you are a huge manipulator. You tested Paul just so he would prove your insecurities wrong."

I replied, "Don't we all? Doesn't every woman and man do things to manipulate to get what we want?"

"Yes," she replied, "but they are not awake to it, so they can't change it yet. Now you are awake. Now you are going to be able to stop yourself from testing Paul in order to make yourself feel better. Jenny, did you ever think from day one you could have sat down and simply said, 'I'm going through these weird emotions since I've moved in, and I don't feel like I belong here. I want to feel at home, but I'm having a hard time"?

Yeah, why didn't I? I totally could have. Why couldn't I simply state my insecurities? I've realized that it's hard to express our insecurities to our men when we really just want to be adored, loved, and lusted over by them. We want to look like the perfect mates, not insecure hot messes. Well, looking at my own crap, I could see so clearly that I'd done this with more than just the furniture in my life. I mean, if we haven't felt desired by our man in a long time, haven't we all dropped a, "This guy hit on me at the store," instead of just saying, "I'm not feeling like you find me sexy anymore"? We are masters of manipulation.

So, I hope some of you saw yourself in my story. I've gotten so much more self-aware, but I still bust myself from time to time. Let's just remember to examine our behavior and ask the question, "What do I really want? What do I really fear that's causing me to act this way?" And then sit down with your man and tell him. It could save you years of manipulation.

33

The Making of a Polish Porn Star

worked in a Polish grocery store selling Polish sausage to Polish people for five years of my life. I was half Polish, so I sort of connected with them. We didn't just sell Polish sausage, this store was unique. We sold porn magazines, too. (Polish people really know how to party!) I was only a teenager, so it was really awkward when men would come in and buy the magazines. "Four links of sausage and *Lip Lust* magazine," they would bark. I would get so angry having to dig through the rack to find their stupid porn, it made me sick. I threw it in their bag and damned their sausage to hell. Ironically, when it was slow, I would glance at the magazines to see what my vagina actually looked like, considering they show angles women never actually see on themselves.

The one magazine that made me a little curious was *Playboy*. Those girls didn't seem like whores, even though I was certain they had sold their souls to the devil. The month I was looking at had Anna Nicole Smith as the centerfold. I remember thinking, "Well, her thighs aren't perfect. I could maybe pull something like this off." Then I quickly put the magazine away, shocked I could ever even have thought that I could do something so disgusting.

A week later I was in front of my garage with a Polaroid camera, taking pictures of myself for modeling agencies. I sent a picture to every agency in downtown Chicago that was a legitimate agency for commercial work. Out of the seventy agencies I sent my picture to, only one called back. I took the bus downtown and stared out the window, dreaming of the fame and fortune that I was sure this commercial agent was going to offer me. I sat down with her and showed her my multiple Polaroids of fancy poses I did in front of my garage door. She immediately laughed and told me to get a bartending job.

I sat there dumbfounded. Did she know I'd spent two weeks' worth of my Polish sausage job money on this outfit? Did she know what I'd told all of my friends and family back in my neighborhood? I told them I was going to Hollywood! I walked out of her office defeated, resigned to a life of serving men sausage and porn. At that moment I looked up and saw the Playboy building. I stared at the giant metal bunny dominating Chicago's skyline and thought, Maybe I'll just go talk to somebody there. Just talk. As I walked across the street and entered the building, I had visions of my mom crying and holding my leg, screaming the Lord's Prayer. I thought of my dad working three jobs to put his four girls through Catholic school and how he would be so disappointed if I posed nude. Yet I watched my hand reach for the elevator button, and I stepped inside. When the doors opened, I arrived in the lobby of *Playboy* magazine. I approached the receptionist as if I knew what the hell I was doing. "Hi, I'm just inquiring as to how girls get chosen for *Playboy*." The receptionist told me, "Well, they don't just walk in. We receive over one hundred thousand pictures a year in the mail. You have to submit." I pictured myself posing naked in front of my garage door and realized how horrible my own pictures would turn out. I thanked her and began to walk away. I was so grateful it was a dead end. I wasn't cut out to be a nude model anyway. As the elevator doors opened to take me back to Poland, I heard a voice say, "Excuse me, are you asking about becoming a Playmate?" I turned around to see an executive in a suit. "Um, yeah," I replied.

"Well, we don't normally do this, but we have a photo session going on right now, so if you're comfortable putting on a bikini, we can take some test photos."

People have crossroads in their lives, and before me was

a huge one. I come from good stock—have I mentioned I am Catholic? How could I even consider posing naked when I'd missed maybe three masses in my entire life? "Okay," my mouth said. And I followed this man back into a studio, where I watched my body put on a bikini. How the hell am I here? I kept thinking. I was just on a city bus an hour ago, and now I'm putting a bikini on at *Playboy* magazine. I walked out and stood in front of the camera and began to pose like I was getting a mug shot taken. I couldn't move. I just turned left profile, and then I turned right. The photographer shouted thanks, and I ran out the door as fast as I possibly could. The entire bus ride home, all I could think about was how stupid I was for going there, and how I should start to fill out applications for bartending as fast as possible.

When I walked in the door, I whispered to my sister what I'd just done. She was shocked. My family was so Catholic that we had a statue of Mother Mary that was four feet tall in our living room window. My mom allowed strangers to come in and pray whenever they wanted. I have three aunts that are nuns, two uncles that are priests. We couldn't get any more Catholic short of being the pope. Ya dig? Anyway, I told my sister to calm the hell down because there wasn't a chance in hell that I would get it. There were 100,000 girls vying for a twelve-girl slot. *Ring-ring*, I answered the phone, and it was *Playboy*, telling me that I was going to be Miss October! I'm not kidding. I had just walked in the door. Either they were desperate, or I was destined to become Chicago's Polish porn star. I hung up the phone in shock. I told my sister, and she looked at me like I had just been sentenced to death. "Mom and Dad are going to kill you. Kill you. Kill you. You need to run away." As I paced my bedroom, which was as big as a closet, I realized that this was my ticket out of the barrio. I knew I wasn't a sexy, sultry girl, but I had confidence in myself to *fake* that I was a sexy and sultry girl.

I devised a plan: I would take $2,000 out of my $20,000 paycheck and send my parents on a cruise the week the magazine came out. It seemed like a genius idea at the time. So I went off to the *Playboy* studios and started my first day of posing in my birthday suit. They had me start off in a robe and slowly undress every hour. I felt so weird, uncomfortable, and cold. How often do you stand completely naked in a room full of men? Um . . . never. So, I kept telling myself, Fake it, Jenny, fake it. I tightened up my tummy and arched my back. I got some ooohs and ahhhs, so at least I knew I wasn't making a complete ass out of myself. "Okay," the photographer said, "Off with the undies."

Shit, really, it was time. Boobs are one thing, but a girl's nether regions are precious cargo. In the sexiest possible way I took my panties off and proceeded to strike poses while still covering my crotch with my hands. "Um, Jenny, put your hands on your hips," the photographer politely said. Dammit, he was on to me. Slowly I moved both hands away from my crotch and watched the crew's faces turn confused. Almost as if they'd never seen a crotch like mine; they just kept staring.

I didn't know what to do. I wasn't a man, for Pete's sake; what were they looking at? The photographer called the makeup artist and whispered in her ear. What was he saying to her? Put makeup on my ugly parts? The suspense was killing me!

The makeup artist finally came over and said, "You have the most pubic hair we have ever seen on a girl that has come in here. You've never even shaved, have you?" "Um, no, I didn't know I was supposed to." "Have you ever trimmed?" she asked with a repulsed look on her face. "No," I said with a quiver in my voice. "I'm Polish, I think we're just naturally hairy." The makeup artist turned around and shouted to the whole room, "She's Polish, that's why she is so hairy!" I almost died. I was standing there in the most vulnerable state, and this woman had just shouted that I had roadkill on my canooter. The photographer brought his lighting grip friend over for a closer look. They squatted down, staring and waving their hands across my crotch to see how the light reflected on it, for what felt like an eternity. Finally the photographer said, "Let's just light the hell out of this thing."

This thing? Oh my God, it was roadkill! He looked at the makeup artist. "Get your hairbrush and fluff it up. It's going in all different directions." The makeup artist pulled a giant paddle hairbrush out of her bag and started brushing up and down with strong strokes. She looked at me oddly. "Guess I can't use this brush anymore."

Oh, the horror, the misery. How does one pose sexy when you feel like you're wearing a dead squirrel? Fake it, fake it, that's how. I started pretending I was pretty hot. How would a hot chick pose? Not a clue. I kept doing dumb moves until they finally said, "Let's just do some butt shots now." Butt shots?! Whew, I thought. I can just turn around and cry while they take pictures of my butt. So I turned around and stood there, thinking the worst was over. It wasn't. The photographer said, "Um, Jenny, you have to bend over and then try to turn your face to the lens while sticking your butt towards the lens, too." I felt like such a dork. I did what he said and bent over and heard, "Whoa." Not a good whoa, but a "You thought the front was bad" kind of whoa. Another surprise. "Look at all that hair that's coming from her butt."

What?! I had no idea my butt was as hairy as my crotch. I didn't even know I had hair on my exit door. "Let's light that chunk of hair coming out of her butt," he said.

"*Somebody kill me!*" is what I kept saying to myself. The photographer proceeded to make me stay in the bent-over position for forty-five minutes while he lit my butt-hole hair. Finally, after a twelve-hour day, the shoot came to an end. I was exhausted.

The week the magazine came out was a disaster. As planned, I sent my parents on a cruise to Mexico so they would miss our house getting burned down by the neighborhood. Moments after their flight left, I received a phone call from my uncle, who said he'd just read in the newspaper that a Catholic girl named Jenny McCarthy had posed nude for *Playboy*. I said, "Ummmmmmm, yeah, that's me." He started screaming at the top of his lungs. He told me that I was going to burn in hell and that I had shamed my whole family. My body started trembling because I knew he was right. I was going to burn in hell, and I had shamed my whole family. What had I done?! Things went downhill the rest of the week: my house was covered in toilet paper, and my sisters, who were still at my alma mater, were tortured by the girls there. I couldn't imagine what my parents were going to do to me. Five days later they walked in the door with smiles on their glowing faces. My sister sat them down and told them what I'd done, because we all knew I would have been murdered on the spot.

My dad took it well. My mom, on the other hand, not so well. She reacted by bursting into tears and running into her bedroom. She told my sisters that at least she had three other daughters to love. *Ouch! Damn!* That's not something you want to hear from your mom. She had a breakdown, and so did I. It felt like the world was crashing down on me, and I didn't know how to save myself. Then our eighty-year-old next-door neighbor Ruth came over and talked to my mom. She said, "Linda, who cares what anybody thinks? She's your daughter, and that's that. She's a good girl, and I think she looks beautiful." My mom only needed to hear one outside perspective to turn her thinking around. She came to me and said, I hate what you did, but I love you and will stand by you. I hugged her and cried. I told her to have faith in me. I was gonna get to Hollywood and become famous and do something good with my fame. Looking back now, we talk about that time in our lives. After all the autism activism work I have done, I have made my mom more proud than ever. She says I'm her hero, but to many others back home I will always just be the hairiest Polish porn star from Chicago.

34

Brad Pitt

met Brad Pitt once at a party, just after he had broken up with Gwyneth Paltrow. (He's going to kill me
for telling this story, but he's so busy with his fifteen children I highly doubt he's going to do anything
about it.) We were at some Hollywood Christmas party that
movie producers like to throw in their backyards every year.
These parties are painful to go to and are usually more like
keggers in college than fancy parties. Mainly because they
don't have sponsors like a movie premiere; they are fork-
ing out their own cash to wine and dine, and it's obvious
they spend it only on booze. Anyway, I was there with my

girlfriend, who had that disease I'm sure all of you have heard of, I-leave-my-friend-at-every-party syndrome. It's amazing to witness the disease in full outbreak. One second my friend is next to me, a guy approaches, and the next second, poof! She's gone. Not to be found until the next day, when the disease subsides.

I found myself walking through the party alone but pretending to do that thing where you look left and right as you walk, like you're actually looking for someone. I was on my fourth lap when a guy said, "Can I help you find whoever you are looking for?" I laughed and said, "Oh no, I'm looking for the bathroom." Good cover, idiot.

The guy showed me where the bathroom was, and I headed toward it. Los Angeles wannabe actresses, a semi-actor that I thought I recognized from the third lead in a sitcom, and band guys were all crunched into a hallway waiting for the bathroom. I stood there listening to the "I'm gonna make it in this town" dialogue, wondering why the hell I didn't just leave. Just when I'd finally had enough, I turned around to get the hell out when Brad Pitt joined the line. I casually smiled and spun back around, hoping I didn't seem like a total dork. How do you not geek out on a guy like that? He was wearing a beanie and looked as if he had skipped a couple days shaving. I wanted to shove my tongue down his throat, but I controlled myself and decided to just bask in his scent. I guessed his cologne pretty quickly. You might have heard of it before, it's called marijuana. I didn't care if he was a pothead. He talked openly about it in many interviews, and his honesty turned me on even more. Hell, he could be blind and deaf with no arms and legs. (Well, maybe just one arm. I would definitely need one arm. Okay. A finger.)

The thing about celebs is, you almost need to be one to understand the science of picking one up. Rule number one is, you never tell a celeb that you are a really big fan if you ever hope to sleep with him or her. I've run away from many men who had said that to me. So, what did I do in this bathroom line? I ignored him. I was hoping he was checking out my butt, but people kept talking to him, so the chances were slim. Jeez, leave the guy alone, I kept thinking as I was obnoxiously bending over to pick up the lipstick I had purposely dropped on the ground. Then I heard a familiar voice talking to Brad. I turned around, and saw it was the guy who showed me the way to the bathroom. He told Brad not to wait in this line, that he could go to the room upstairs. The guy caught me looking at him and clearly felt bad that he had steered me to the line with all the normal folk; he asked if I wanted to use that one, too. Brad looked at me, and I kept my focus on the guy and smiled. Then I casually responded with, "Yeah, that'd be great." So the three of us headed to the bathroom, and I stared at Brad's butt the entire time he walked up the stairs. How does he dress like he doesn't care, yet clothing hangs over each buttock like it's making love to it? God, I wanted to bite it. We made it to the bathroom, and Brad went in first, leaving me to talk to the guy that showed us the VIP bathroom.

"My name is Noah, by the way," he said.

"Nice to meet you, I'm Jenny," I replied.

I could tell the guy took a little liking to me, so I gave him a little flirt-talk to keep the conversation going. But all I could do was imagine that Brad Pitt's penis was exposed four feet from my body. I had flashes in my head of being the first woman in the world convicted for rape, and women everywhere in the world cheering me on for doing so.

Then I heard the sounds of flushing and water running and the door opened. Oh, no, I thought, I don't have a plan to stop him. I smiled and walked right past him, cool as a cucumber, into the bathroom and shut the door. Dammit, I thought. There goes my one shot to bone the sexiest man alive. And then I heard Noah striking up a conversation with him. I realized that I had my head plastered to the door while listening to what they were saying instead of peeing. I pulled my pants down, forced out three drops of urine, and quickly wiped. *Flush flush, wash wash.* I opened the door, and it was just Noah standing there waiting for me. I was crushed. I'd blown it.

And then Noah performed a miracle in front of my eyes. "So, Brad just invited me back to his place to hang. Do you want to come with?" Holy shit, this guy has no idea, but he just picked up a rapist and is about to take the rapist to the victim's house. "Yeah, that sounds cool," I said. Noah smiled, and I followed him through the house and out the door. We got to the valet, and that's where we met up with Brad. Noah made the introduction: "Hey, Brad, this is Jenny." My eyes slowly met his, and we shook hands. His voice went into slow motion, "Niiiicceee toooo meeeeeet youuuuuu." Then a girl popped out of nowhere and shouted to us, "Ready to go, our car is here."

Hold on, pussycat, who are you? Who is this creature I must destroy who looks cute as a button dragging my rape victim to a car? Damn. How was I going to try and do anything with a pussy-blocker in the way? The valet opened the car door, and she got into the driver seat and Noah jumped into the passenger seat. I stood there confused as Brad climbed into the back seat, leaving the only place for me . . . in the back seat next to him! Brad must have asked Noah to ask me to come back to his place. The pussy-blocker had to be Noah's girlfriend. Holy crap, Batman! I was dying. I tried to keep cool and just sort of agreed with whatever they were talking about in the car. We pulled up to a very nondescript gate, and it took security all of three seconds to open it. Brad started asking me questions about myself and was very casual about it in a flirty way. We walked into his house, and it looked like it came out of *Architectural Digest*. A butler or something approached us and asked if we wanted a drink. I ordered some vodka with a splash of lemon to calm my nerves. We headed into a den that was dark but cozy. I was seriously pitting out so bad from nerves that I asked to use his bathroom strictly to wipe some of the sweat away. "Yeah, I'll show you where it is," Brad said. Oh, no, I wasn't ready to rape him yet. I couldn't rape someone when I had BO.

We were walking down the hallway, talking about little

shit, when he grabbed me and pushed me against a wall. I stared at him for a second, and then we slowly kissed. The butterflies in my stomach were going berserk. I slid my hands down his back and managed to get one of my hands on his oh-so-fine ass. And yes, ladies and gay men, it was oh-so-fine. We made out for a few minutes, and then I pulled him into the bathroom. I closed the lid of the toilet and made him sit down. I squatted on my knees and slowly started to rub my face on his inner thighs while looking up at him. I was giving it my super-duper naughty face, and just as I was about to unzip his pants . . . the freaking butler shouted that my drink was ready! What an idiot! He ruined the only rape moment I wanted to experience in my life with freaking vodka! Brad snapped out of my love spell and started to get up. I stopped him and said, "Wanna do me in the butt?"

Okay, I can't go on any longer. I faked this whole chapter. Hahaha, sorry. I know, I wish it were real, too. Hahahaha.

35

What Are Friends For?

Well, the real ones hold your hair when you puke, lie to your boyfriend for you, loan you their favorite shirt, pick you up from a one-night stand, listen to your drama; they don't copy your hairstyle, don't gossip about you, they don't flirt with *your* man, they're genuinely happy for you and would defend you in any battle.

The fake friends go to the hair salon and come back saying the hairdresser accidentally gave them the same haircut as yours, they buy the same clothes, get you wasted so they can flirt with your boyfriends, never call to ask how *you* are doing, won't do a McDonald's run when you're hung over, compete with you, are jealous of you, and will talk behind your back the moment you turn around.

My first experience of fake friendship came in eighth grade. A new girl named Joanna Kline moved to our school. We hit it off, and in no time we were meeting boys in back alleys to make out and dry-hump them against garage doors. We were so close in eighth grade that we would force each other to chug vodka to see who would puke green stuff the quickest and then take pictures of each other getting sick. I dropped almost all of my other friends because Joanna told me to. She wanted me all to herself. Sadly, it took less than a year for her demon horns to reveal themselves through her bleached hair.

I went to the mall with my sister one frightful day, and there I spotted Joanna holding hands with a boy that didn't look like her boyfriend. I pulled my sister behind a phone booth (remember those?), and we spent the next ten minutes spying on her indiscretions. I couldn't make out whom she was with, but it wasn't the Italian boy she usually dry-humped. This guy was blond, tan, and wore Cavaricci pants. Wait . . . hold on a second, I thought. That's . . . MY FUCKING BOYFRIEND! I felt my heart chambers rip apart from one another like the Velcro strips on a Nike sneaker. My body started trembling as I saw them move their faces toward one another and lock lips. I looked at my younger sister, whose eyes were as big as saucers; she began to speak to me, but everything went in to slow motion and her

voice sounded all distorted: "Ooooooooooooooooooooohhh-
hhhhhhhhhhhhhh noooooooooooooooooooooooo." I looked
back at my boyfriend and the bitch and did what any girl from
the South Side of Chicago would have done in my place. I
took off running like a bat out of hell. Not away from them.
Oh, no. I took off directly toward them like a bull let out of a
pen. I was a fifty-yard track star and used every piece of talent
I had within me to get there in record speed and knock down
my former best friend going about thirty miles an hour. She
started screaming like a crazy person, so again I did what any
South Side Chicago girl would do. I dragged her by her hair
around the corner and down the stairs near the arcade and
proceeded to beat the shit out of her.

So I'm beating the shit out of Joanna when I hear the mall
police shout, "What the hell is going on?" I got off Joanna and
looked at my boyfriend, who stared at me in awe. He mumbled,
"You really love me." I grabbed his hand, and we took off running away from the police. When we made it to a safe hiding
place, I cried on his shoulder and told him to never ever ever
ever cheat on me again. How stupid is that? He was the one I
should have beaten the shit out of.

Joanna opened my eyes. My first week of high school was
tough. I was scared of making friends because I now knew
firsthand how hard it was to pick out who would be real and
who would turn into a fake backstabbing bitch. I decided to
take my chance on a girl named Krissy, and we hit it off that
first week. Krissy seemed to come from good stock; she was as

poor as I was, so we could relate to wearing hand-me-downs from our older sisters. We seemed to really get along and walked through the hallways of Catholic school giggling and gossiping like we had been friends forever. Sadly, it also only took the evil group of girls in the school one week to decide to target me for destruction. I didn't do anything to provoke it, but I'm guessing my long bleached blond hair made me the perfect choice. Krissy and I did everything to avoid the "Heathers" from seeing us in between classes. It didn't take them too long to figure out my hiding spots, though, and they attacked me with shaving cream pies and punches to the stomach. I even had to endure the bus ride home without Krissy. Just me and the Heathers. They would shout names at me and spit on me, which I realized now was great training for Hollywood. I was so abused in high school that I'm unfazed by any critics or any negative press thanks to the thick skin I had to grow during my teenage years.

So, on this bus ride home, without my friend Krissy, the Heathers decided to sit behind me and talk about my fluffy long bleached Barbie hair like it was the ugliest haystack they had ever seen. I kept praying to God nothing too extreme would happen, but I think God was on a pee break and didn't hear. I started to smell something awful and couldn't figure out what it was. Then a voice inside my head said, *That smells like hair burning.* I put my hand behind my head and felt fire burning my Aqua Net–sprayed locks. I stood up screaming and frantically patted down my hair while everyone on the bus laughed hysterically. I wore my hair in a French braid for the next four months.

What surprised me even more than my hair burning was what happened next; I was walking to class with Krissy, talking about how I had just gotten my period and didn't make it to the bathroom in time to get a tampon. My underwear suffered some damage, so I decided to take them off and put them in my locker. After the next class, I made my way through the hallways with lightning speed to avoid the Heathers.

I turned toward the last wing to make it to Spanish class to find the entire hallway backed up with girls screaming, laughing, and pointing to the wall above the lockers. I couldn't quite make it out, so I pushed through the crowd. As my vision became clear, my whole being (whatever was left of it) came crashing down into the pits of hell. My period underwear was hanging up on the wall with my name and an arrow pointing to it. The only person that knew my combination was Krissy. She had given it to the enemy.

From that day forward I missed so much high school they told my parents that I wouldn't graduate. How could I go to school with the Heathers plotting my demise, and now my very own friend joining the dark side? I was devastated and hurt and prayed college would get easier.

And it did. On my very first day of college, I met a girl named Julie who I knew was the real deal. We went out dancing and drinking and realized that we would be lifelong friends. I'm happy to say that she remains my best friend today. The only thing that's shitty about our friendship is that she still lives in Chicago, and she keeps having babies. I don't know how much longer I can stay friends with her if she keeps blowing her vagina to bits. I mean, seriously Julie, WTF. Get on the pill.

Moving to L.A. would seem like the scariest place to make friends, but fortunately I met up with a couple named Paul and Jackie from Canada soon after I moved here. They are funny and kind and have been at my side throughout Evan's autism and my interesting choice of men over the years. They know the perfect mixture of support and ridicule when I decide to do dumb things like get married or dye my hair black. I will forever be grateful for their real friendship.

Now, celebrity friends are a whole other ball of wax. Many have tried to become friends with me, and I couldn't run faster. Maybe because they reminded me of the Heathers. From an outside perspective one might think my friend Chelsea Handler would be cast as the perfect Heather, but she is anything but in real life. She takes care of her family and friends and even helps out some real losers that I don't approve of. She has put some of the biggest smiles on my face the past few years, and I continue to hold her responsible for continuously breaking my Botox. When I told her I was writing a chapter on real friends, she e-mailed me her thoughts on the subject . . .

"Jenny and I truly fell in love when we both became single, and that's when I realized, I'll always be straight."

So to answer the question, What are friends for? They are the ultimate reflection of yourself. Always surround yourself with people who inspire you and return the favor by giving them the best of you.

36

My Buddhahood

Ending a five-year relationship (a mutual split) made me ask myself some serious questions, like, What's going on with you, girl? You all right? I felt really lost and confused as to what my path was. Life changes are always disorienting, especially when you've imagined yourself either growing old with someone or staying in the same occupation forever. During this transitional period in my life, I had to go back and remind myself of an earlier dream I had of becoming a big-time movie star actress, which obviously didn't come to pass. I envisioned myself on the big screen and getting my Walk of Fame star; instead, I currently hold the record for the most razzies any actress has ever received. I also have fourteen failed sitcom pilots sitting in my drawer. But even though I didn't find success in that career path, I managed to make this book my seventh *New York Times* bestselling book. (Well, I hope this one is also a bestseller.) My point being, even though I felt like the shit really hit the fan in this relationship, I stopped and thought, Hey, maybe not. I've proved it to myself before. This shit could turn into the best-looking shit I've ever seen. I mean, if anyone can turn shit into a rose garden, I think I've got a shot at it!

So off I went! I started to seek some outside help and invested in tarot cards, aura spray, crystals, and psychics to provide some direction. I'm a big believer in this kind of stuff, and it did help, but something was still missing. It felt like I was walking around the rose garden looking at the flowers, when what I needed was the key to get *inside* the garden. Where the hell is the key? I kept wondering. I know it's out there. I've always been a spiritual person, but now I felt like I needed guidance gathering all of my beliefs into one place so that my roses could start manifesting. I wanted to find out who I was without anyone having to explain it to me. I wanted to be able to become less fearful of the future and eventually be ready for love again. But how? I thought. Where do I begin to find answers?

The idea of organized religion wasn't ringing my bell after all the years of Catholic school I endured. Don't get me wrong, Jesus is cool and I dig 'im, but I felt an urge to expand my horizons. When you ask you shall receive, or whatever the hell that saying is. A friend casually mentioned that she was enjoying learning about Buddhism and felt so enlightened by it that she had become a Buddhist. I knew something was going on with her, because over the past few months she just seemed at peace with whatever shit came her way. As she started to describe how much it helped her in detail, I felt the need to ask more questions. Could this be worth trying? I mean, if it *really* worked for her (who used to be one hot mess, I might add), why couldn't I get some of that shit she was on? As I was about to ask my friend some more questions about it, I heard my mom's voice shout inside my head: *They worship a big fat guy who sits down all the time.* So I reworded it and asked, "Why do they pray to Buddha?" She responded, "We don't pray to Buddha. Buddhists don't really have any Buddha statues around the house. Other people just seem to use them for decor, but not usually Buddhists. Buddha is a term for an enlightened state. We all have Buddha in us."

I responded with, "Well, what kind of religion is this if you don't pray to someone?"

She said, "Buddhism is not really a religion. It's more of a philosophy."

I said, "Well, can it turn shit into roses?"

She replied, "Absolutely. Its called turning poison into medicine, but you're calling it turning shit into roses, which is the same thing."

"Well, I got shit right now, and I want roses. I already have plenty of medicine in my cabinets."

She said, "There is no outside force that will make you do anything. Everything comes from within you. You are in charge."

I replied, "If this is true, then why bother praying or worshiping or following any type of philosophy or religion when you can do it all by yourself?"

She said, "I agree. Buddhism just gives me the tools I need to make sure I'm always in charge of my destiny, and chanting in the morning and at night holds me accountable for my progress. When we chant in Buddhism we chant *nam-myho-renge-kyo*, and by saying that, we are allowed to polish our own mirror so we can see ourselves clearly. We are chanting / 'praying' / believing in ourselves. Transforming our fear into courage."

Transforming fear into courage was what I was longing for. Being alone in the house was scary, wondering how I would pay all the bills by myself was scary, thinking of growing old with no one at my side was scary, and hoping Evan was okay with the transition was scary. I figured, "What the hell? Why not give some Buddhism a whirl?" As long as I can still think Jesus is a cool dude and Buddhism just gives me the tools to manifest change within me, it all sounded kinda cool.

I've been practicing for a little over three months now, and I have managed to take my shit and not only use it as fertilizer to grow roses but to cultivate the most beautiful lotus flower within me. I don't feel lost now when life gives me a hiccup. I know what to do. I chant and I get stronger every day. Before I would have said, "Thanks, Buddha, for this new direction in my life." But now I know better. The chubby dude that sits around all the time would say, "No, thank yourself. I'm just holding the mirror."

There seem to be two phases of moving on. The one where we pick up our lives, create new routines, heal past resentments, and love ourselves. The second phase is being ready to find love in a companion again. As I write this, I'm only in phase one. But I know already that as far as my future love life is concerned, my expectations will be very high. I don't mean I have a laundry list of superficial things I need from a man—like doing whatever I say, or letting me have the remote control. When I say expectations, I mean baseline qualities I know I deserve: a man who respects women, a guy who enjoys life, someone who wants to spiritually grow with me and has enormous amounts of self-love. Basically, what I'm saying is that I'm raising the bar in terms of my future guy only because my *own* bar will be raised before I ever meet him. I intend to know who I am, love myself, feel okay on my own, and not need anything from my partner to make me feel better. Can't wait to meet him. Hope he doesn't have a mullet.

P.S. Go to www.sgi.org for more info on how to turn your shit into roses and follow me on Twitter @ JennyMcCarthy.

Acknowledgments

In no particular order, these are the brave souls who have stood by me while I continue to make an ass out of myself.

Leigh Brecheen

Erwin More

Jennifer Rudolph Walsh

Jennifer Barth

Lauren Auslander

Paul Greenberg

Julie Ribordy

Chelsea Handler

Becky (Jennifer) Obirek

Brad Cafarelli

Thank you for helping me bust out another awesome book!

About the Author

Model, comedian, actress, and activist Jenny McCarthy is the author of the *New York Times* bestsellers *Belly Laughs*, *Baby Laughs*, and *Louder Than Words*, among others. The former host of MTV's hugely popular dating show *Singled Out*, McCarthy began her career as a *Playboy* magazine model before launching a high-profile comedic television and film career. Most recently, she has appeared on the shows *My Name Is Earl*, *Two and a Half Men*, and *Chuck*. She has been featured on virtually every television talk show, from *Larry King Live*, *The View*, *Ellen*, and Letterman to Conan O'Brien, *Hannity & Colmes*, and Howard Stern. She is also a frequent guest on the *Oprah Winfrey Show*.

In addition to her work in the world of healing and preventing autism, she is the cocreator, with practicing speech language pathologist Sarah Clifford Scheflen, of Teach2Talk, a series of DVDs for children. She has also served as a spokesperson for post-pregnancy weight loss for Weight Watchers. Her unique combination of intelligence, sex appeal, and humor has landed her on the covers of magazines as diverse as *People*, *Playboy*, *Rolling Stone*, and *Self*; recently, she was featured in *Time*.

Born in Chicago, McCarthy currently resides in Los Angeles with her son, Evan.